ALSO BY BO BOSHERS

Student Ministry for the 21st Century

Doing Life with God, Volumes 1 and 2

Becoming a Contagious Christian, Youth Edition

Taking Your Relationship
with God to a New Level

Bo Boshers

ZONDERVAN™

GRAND RAPIDS, MICHIGAN 49530 USA

We want to hear from you. Please send your comments about this book to us in care of zreview@zondervan.com. Thank you.

ZONDERVAN™

G-Force
Copyright © 2003 by Willow Creek Association

Requests for information should be addressed to:
Zondervan, *Grand Rapids, Michigan 49530*

ISBN 0-310-24446-3

All Scripture quotations, unless otherwise indicated, are taken from the *Holy Bible, New Living Translation,* copyright © 1996. Used by permission of Tyndale House Publishers, Inc., Wheaton, IL 60189. All rights reserved.

Scripture quotations marked TNIV are taken from the *Holy Bible: Today's New International Version™*. Copyright © 2001 by International Bible Society. Used by permission of Zondervan. All rights reserved.

Scripture quotations marked NKJV are taken from the *Holy Bible: New King James Version*. Copyright © 1984. Used by permission of Thomas Nelson, Inc. All rights reserved.

Interior design by Holli Leegwater

Printed in the United States of America

05 06 07 08 09 /❖ DC/ 10 9 8 7 6

This book is dedicated to all the shepherd leaders who understand the importance of building authentic community in small groups with this generation. I applaud your commitment to provide a healthy spiritual, emotional, and relational environment for students by not trying to fix, change, or judge them. Truth spoken in love, correction given in love, reproof received in the spirit of love, and grace given in love will have a life-changing impact on this generation.

My prayer is that this book will assist you as you lead this generation down a path of full devotion to Christ. May God bless you.

dedication

gContents

1 Fully Devoted

2 GRACE, Part 1: A True Gift

3 GRACE, Part 2: Sharing the Gift

a word TO STUDENTS ...

As a pastor, coworker, and parent, the world of students at Willow Creek is a matter of urgent importance to me. No one carries the history and passion for that world with more enthusiasm than Bo Boshers. I wish you could experience his energy personally, but until you do this resource is a great asset. It has the potential to fuel enormous growth for any student with an open heart. When I think about the kind of planet you are inheriting, I am particularly grateful for the promise that with God's presence you do not face today or tomorrow alone.

Bo has served the local church effectively in the area of student ministries for many years and has for the past seven years trained, equipped, and cheered on student ministries and their leaders at churches all over the world. He is uniquely gifted and qualified to serve you as a spiritual guide.

You are, right now, a potent force in your world—for better or for worse. And in the years to come, your impact will only grow greater. Many students I meet have a deep passion to know God, grow in faith, serve the poor—but they want to know *how*. In *G-Force*, Bo lays out how discipleship can become a concrete reality. In a world of guilt, you can be immersed in *grace*. In place of stagnation, you can know *growth*. Instead of isolation, you can live in *groups* and community. You can discover emerging *gifts* that will impact your church and world, and in an era of mall-culture, you can be a *good steward* at the beginning of your financial life.

G-Force shows how you can become the difference-maker God made you to be. As you walk through daily devotions and talk in small groups about what you're learning, you'll begin to see what God has planned for your life and you will gain courage to take bold steps to become more like Christ.

a word TO STUDENT MINISTRY LEADERS AND VOLUNTEERS ...

As I think about this generation of young students, I am particularly grateful to student ministry workers who have devoted themselves to teaching, training, and loving the young men and women who will one day inherit this world. After all, what could matter more than this next generation of Christ-followers? *G-Force* provides a clear path to help you equip and shape students into the Christ-followers who will become our future. So read on, and get ready to see your student ministry transformed!

John Ortberg

I am indebted to many people who made significant contributions to the development of *G-Force*. These include:

Mickey Maudlin, a gifted writer who captured my thoughts and made them clear and effective for training students to become fully devoted followers of Christ.

Christine Anderson, director of product development at the WCA and, more important, my friend. This project would not have been possible without your gifts and direction. Thank you for helping my weaknesses become strengths.

Lynette Rubin, my longtime assistant, for her patience and organizational skills in making changes—over and over again. I could not have done this project without you.

John Ortberg, a gifted teaching pastor, for his support and encouragement, and for his commitment to teaching and training all believers in the biblical truths of spiritual formation and transformation.

Darren DeGraaf, Scott Rubin, and Jeff Vanderstelt, student ministry workers, for offering insights and expertise to insure that *G-Force* is relevant to the needs of junior and senior high school students.

Brandy Ogata, Pat McAndrew, Mike Lueth, and the WCA Student Ministries staff, for their support and can-do attitudes.

Hundreds of student ministry workers around the world who are part of The NET—the WCA's online provider of student ministry resources and training. Thank you for your advice and insights as *G-Force* was developed.

Willow Creek Association staff, for their commitment to providing vision, training, and resources to church leaders around the world. It is a privilege to be on the same team with you.

Zondervan staff, including John Raymond, Alicia Mey, and Angela Scheff for their support and expertise in publishing *G-Force* with excellence.

My wonderful family—my wife and best friend, Gloria, my daughter and princess, Tiffany, my two sons and partners, Brandon and Trevor. Your prayers, support, and encouragement mean more to me than words can say. I love you with all my heart.

acknowledgments

Five-G Living

what DOES IT MEAN TO BE A STRONG CHRISTIAN?

Be careful how you answer that question. You could find yourself following rules and pursuing activities that make your spiritual life boring—or worse, harmful. On the other hand, if you answer the question another way, you could end up on an exciting adventure—a life of freedom and fulfillment, of becoming a "difference-maker" to be used by God.

G-Force was written for your generation of young Christ-followers who want to pursue authentic spiritual transformation. It involves having a real, life-changing experience with God. Each week you will be challenged to think about what you really believe and learn how to experience a deeper relationship with God and with others. You may find that being spiritual is not what you thought, and that being a Christ-follower is more exciting and rewarding than you could ever have imagined!

how DOES IT WORK?

So how does spiritual transformation work? It starts with a group of people who will commit to going on this journey together. While it is certainly possible to go through this guide on your own, it is designed to be a group journey because God often teaches us best in groups.

If you have a group leader, there are Leader's Notes in the back for any preparation work or guidance that may be needed for the studies.

Each session begins with a Group Study that introduces a subject to be explored. The Group Study is followed by five Daily Devotions that everyone in the group does on his or her own during the time in between the Group Studies.

The topics focus on the Five Gs—Grace, Growth, Groups, Gifts, and Good Steward-ship—with two sessions devoted to each "G." These Gs are markers in our spiritual journey to show us the progress we have made in our becoming more like Christ. The journey will not be complete by the end of this book. Spiritual transformation takes a lifetime. But the Five Gs are what you will need for this lifelong journey.

Be sure you have a good modern translation of the Bible, such as the *New Living Translation, Today's New International Version,* the *New Revised Standard Version,* or one of the many others. Choose a Bible you'll feel comfortable writing in. You'll be invited to really wrestle with the issues in each study and part of that will involve underlining or highlighting passages in your Bible.

It is up to you to make this journey successful. Your group leader is not there to lecture you. The questions are open-ended and need your participation to work. And not only do you discuss questions, each Group Study and Daily Devotion has an Experience It Yourself component where you get to practice applying what you are studying.

If you want to learn how living the Christian life can be a daily adventure, *G-Force* is just for you.

introduction

GROUP ONE

g₁

Fully Devoted

You are beginning a journey of spiritual transformation. A *transformation* is not merely changing something about yourself, like growing your hair long. It is changing *natures,* our inner selves. Transformation is like a larva in a cocoon. In time that same larva becomes a butterfly, and its entire nature is changed. That is what it is like when we choose to follow Jesus. The goal of this study is to become more like Jesus—to be transformed from the inside out. In the coming weeks, the goal is for all of us to become more like Jesus. You will explore the key qualities that characterize a fully devoted follower of Jesus, which are called the Five Gs—Grace, Growth, Groups, Gifts, and Good Stewardship. The Five Gs are markers along the lifelong journey of transformation that help you assess your progress. These sessions will teach you how to use the Five-G markers to stay on the right path of full devotion. Following Jesus is always an exciting and fulfilling adventure. So let's begin!

opening UP

1. Describe the most *spiritual* person you can imagine. What would that person be like?

2. Now describe the most *fun* person you can imagine. What would that person be like?

3. What do you think it would have been like to hang out with Jesus when he walked the earth? Would he have been more like your ideal spiritual person or your ideal fun person?

read TOGETHER

Read these verses aloud and discuss them as a group:

explore TOGETHER

1. According to John's first letter, how should we measure what it means to be "godly" or "spiritual"?

>> **1 john 2:6**
Those who say they live in God should live their lives as Christ did.

>> **colossians 3:17**
Whatever you do or say, let it be as a representative of the Lord Jesus.

>> **mark 12:29–31**
[Jesus speaking] "The most important commandment is this: 'Hear, O Israel! The Lord our God is the one and only Lord. And you must love the Lord your God with all your heart, all your soul, all your mind, and all your strength.' The second is equally important: 'Love your neighbor as yourself.' No other commandment is greater than these."

2. According to the apostle Paul's letter to the Colossians (a local church in Colosse, a city in what is now the country Turkey), in what part of our lives should we strive to be "spiritual" like Jesus?

3. If we are to imitate how Jesus lived, then what do Jesus' words in Mark tell us about what guiding values shaped his life?

discuss TOGETHER

1. From God's perspective, your spiritual life is simply your whole life—every minute and detail of it. There is no part of your life that is not God's or where you don't have to live by God's standard: to imitate Jesus in what you do and say. Reread Paul's words in Colossians 3:17 on page 16. Have each person pick one activity below, and explain how it would be different if they were to live like Jesus would:

>> waking up

>> greeting those you see first in the morning

>> eating

>> how you act at school

>> listening to music

>> playing sports

>> spending time with friends

>> doing household tasks

>> using your computer

>> doing homework

>> interacting with your family

>> going to sleep

Based on your discussion, where do you need to be challenged to think about how you live each moment as someone who has Jesus as their leader?

2. Take a moment and have someone write on a white board or flip chart all the rules you've been taught about spirituality (for example, to have a daily quiet time, read the Bible, and so on).

Now have the same person write down another list marked "real spirituality." Under that heading, have the person write "freedom." Since spirituality is really a love relationship with God that is expressed by loving others rather than following a list of rules, discuss the real motivations for doing some of the "rules" in the first list.

3. The best way to see if we are imitating Jesus is to ask ourselves this simple question: Am I becoming more loving toward God and others? Is this true for you? Have you become more loving since you became a Christian? How would those who know you best—family members, teachers, coaches, friends—answer that question?

experience IT TOGETHER

Everyone should read to themselves the Ten Core Values (page 19) and the promise below. After you finish reading the statement silently, sign and date the pledge as a commitment to help each other on this journey of spiritual transformation.

Now choose someone to be your accountability partner. This is the person you will encourage and pray for to stay committed, and they will do the same for you. You will ask each other how the Daily Devotions and spiritual exercises are going. Exchange email addresses and phone numbers and commit to contacting each other often.

MY PROMISE

I,

_____

[your name], promise to explore what it means to become a fully devoted Christ-follower and enter into a journey of spiritual transformation. I pledge to do my best to fully participate in the Daily Devotions and in the eleven Group Studies. I will do my best to open up my heart, soul, and mind to what God wants to teach me on this journey.

_____ _____

Signature   Date

>> **Spiritual Transformation. . .**

2 is a journey, not a destination.

5 involves my whole life (not just the so-called "spiritual" parts).

4 involves those practices, experiences, and relationships that help me be more like Jesus.

7 is not just something I do on my own but involves being part of a community.

1 is essential, not optional, for Christ-followers.

8 is not dependent on my skills or abilities— it's available to everyone.

3 is God's work, but needs my participation.

10 is best measured by how well I love God and others.

6 can happen any time, any place (no restrictions!).

9 is not "one size fits all" but is customized to my personality, circum-stances, and gifts.

community TIME

Talk about what your hopes are for this group during this journey. What do you personally hope to learn and experience in the upcoming weeks? Do you have any doubts or fears about this?

After everyone shares their hopes and personal goals, take out a candle and light it. The light represents God's presence (see John 1:9, where Jesus is described as the "true light" who "gives light to everyone") as you commit yourself to this eleven-week process. Pray that God blesses this adventure and that everybody's goals would be fulfilled. Also ask God to give each person the type of spiritual transformation described in the Ten Core Values. Go around the group and read out loud the Ten Core Values. Then close in prayer, asking God to give you this kind of transformation in your life.

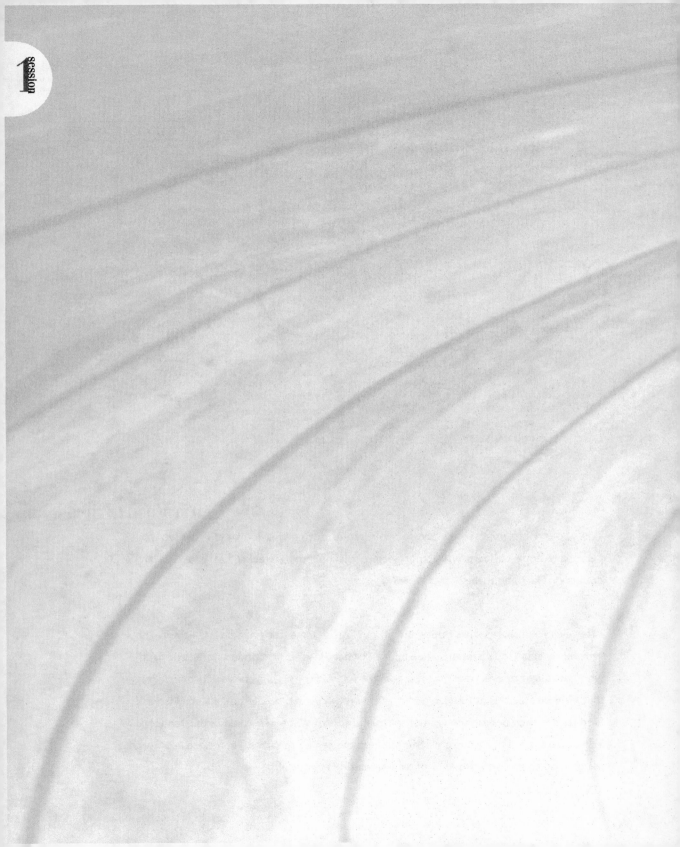

S¹

Fully Devoted

If someone came up to you and asked, "What does it mean to have a spiritual life?" what would you say? Finding out the right answer to that question and how to live it out is what this book is all about. What we mean by having "spiritual life" determines what path we will take in our journey with God. If we have the same perspective God does, then we will follow the right path and become a fully devoted follower of Jesus. If we have a different perspective than God's, then we will choose the wrong path and possibly waste time pursuing activities that don't help us pursue spiritual transformation or that could possibly even harm us. So what is your spiritual life? The following Daily Devotions will define spiritual life and help you live it as Jesus would.

Devotion One

d 1   Giving Your All

The Bible passages from the Group Study helped us to start to answer the question about the true meaning of spirituality: to live our lives "as Christ did" and "as a representative of the Lord Jesus." Let's look more closely at these verses to see how exactly we are to run the race in which God has placed us.

see FOR YOURSELF

Highlight or underline these verses in your Bible:

ask YOURSELF

1. Considering what John (1 John right) says about how a Christ-follower should live, do you claim to be one? Why or why not?

2. Why do you think we are to live our lives "as a representative of the Lord Jesus"? How might your life be different if you lived this way?

>> **1 john 2:6**
Those who say they live in God should *live their lives as Christ did.*

>> **colossians 3:17**
Whatever you do or say, let it be as a representative of the Lord Jesus.

>> **mark 12:29–31**
[Jesus speaking] "The most important commandment is this: 'Hear, O Israel! The Lord our God is the one and only Lord. And you must *love the Lord your God with all your heart, all your soul, all your mind, and all your strength.'* The second is equally important: 'Love your neighbor as yourself.' No other commandment is greater than these."

3. Describe the extent of the love we are to have for God according to Jesus in Mark 12. What is left of ourselves after we have loved with all our heart, soul, mind, and strength?

Someone who is fully devoted is one who is committed to knowing Jesus more intimately, and to live as if he was in your place—thinking as he thinks, speaking as he speaks, walking as he walks. To what extent does this reflect your own life and commitment? In the space below, write a letter to God, sharing some of your doubts and those areas of your life that you know you will struggle with as you journey towards a life that looks like Jesus' life did. Let him know your desire is to be a fully devoted follower of his. Ask for God's help to become more like Jesus in the coming weeks. Include your thoughts and feelings in the letter.

Tomorrow at school, after each class, ask yourself if you are becoming more loving toward God and others. Wear a rubber band around your wrist (or over your watch) to remind you to seek to become more like Jesus. See how this affects your actions for the day.

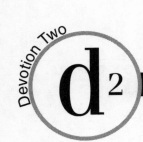

Devotion Two

d² A Marathon, Not a Sprint

Becoming a fully devoted follower does not happen quickly. It takes time—in fact, it's a lifelong journey. What's important is that we stay in the race, knowing that God will get us to the finish line.

see FOR YOURSELF

Highlight or underline these verses in your Bible:

>> **1 corinthians 9:24–26**
Remember that in a race everyone runs, but only one person gets the prize. *You also must run in such a way that you will win.* All athletes practice strict self-control. They do it to win a prize that will fade away, but we do it for an eternal prize. So I run straight to the goal with purpose in every step.

>> **2 timothy 4:7**
I have *fought a good fight*, I have *finished the race*, and I have *remained faithful*.

>> **hebrews 12:1–2**
Since we are surrounded by such a huge crowd of witnesses [spiritual examples] to the life of faith, *let us strip off every weight that slows us down, especially the sin that so easily hinders our progress.* And let us run with endurance the race that God has set before us. We do this by keeping our eyes on Jesus, on whom our faith depends from start to finish.

ask YOURSELF

1. All three passages describe the Christian life as a race. How is being a Christ-follower like being in a race? What do you think is the prize that Paul is referring to?

2. What are the three accomplishments Paul mentions in the 2 Timothy passage on page 24? Underline them. What could these three action steps mean in your life?

3. According to the Hebrews passage on page 24, what are we to strip off in order to run the race? What strategy is recommended for how to race with endurance?

think FOR YOURSELF

How are you doing in the race God has marked out for your life? What do you need to strip off? Where do you need to persevere? In the space below, write what you need to do to get ready for your race. Then write a prayer letting God know where you need help. Ask him to use the coming studies and devotions to help you run the race he's set before you.

experience IT YOURSELF

Take a short walk (if you can't do this, just close your eyes and imagine taking a walk with God). During the walk, talk with God about your life. Let the walk remind you of the race God has set before you. Remember two things: It is not a sprint and God is always there walking next to you.

Devotion Three

d³   **Graduation**

It's your graduation day and you are very excited. All your friends and family are there to celebrate your big day. When your name is announced, you get up to get your diploma—graduating from first grade. Seems like the last eighteen years just flew by. But you did it, you are now a second grader.

What's wrong with this picture? You're not supposed to be eighteen years old when you enter second grade. Something went wrong.

see FOR YOURSELF

Highlight or underline these verses in your Bible:

ask YOURSELF

1. What does Proverbs 22:6 say about learning about God when you are young?

>> **proverbs 22:6**
Teach your children to choose the right path, and when they are older, they will remain upon it.

>> **proverbs 20:11**
Even children are known by the way they act, whether their conduct is pure and right.

>> **1 corinthians 13:11**
When I was a child, I spoke and thought and reasoned as a child does. But *when I grew up, I put away childish things.*

2. According to Proverbs 20:11, how does our conduct reveal who we are?

3. Based on 1 Corinthians 13:11, how is being a Christ-follower like growing up? What childish things do you have to "put away"?

Think about how long you've been a Christ-follower. (If you still have not made this decision, talk to your youth leader about the questions you still may have.) The day you became a Christian, regardless of how old you were, you were like a child. Each week, month, and year, you should be growing in your relationship with Jesus. Just like the story of the eighteen-year-old graduating from first grade, something is wrong if we are not progressing in our lives as Christ-followers.

In the list below, check off the major markers in your Christian life. (If you have not become a follower of Jesus, summarize your life journey so far.)

I was _____ years old when I became a follower of Jesus.

Since becoming a Christian I have become more like Christ in the following ways (check all that apply):

_____ I have more compassion for my friends who don't know Jesus.

_____ I have shared my faith with someone I care about.

_____ I have a greater desire to become more like Jesus.

_____ I look forward to spending time alone with God.

_____ I am more loving with my family and friends.

_____ I have a greater desire to learn and grow together with other believers.

_____ I am more willing to help and serve others.

_____ I believe everything I own is a gift from God and belongs to him.

List other ways you have become more like Christ:

Using the list above as a reference, write below the two or three ways you would most like to focus on to become more like Jesus in the coming weeks.

experience IT YOURSELF

Get some crayons and paper and color a picture using your nondominant hand (for example, use your left hand if you are right-handed). Let this picture represent staying a child, and not maturing as a Christ-follower. Afterward, pray and ask God to help you put away childish things, to help you mature as a Christian believer. Now sign and date the picture you drew. Write at the bottom of it: "It's graduation time." Display this picture in your room to remind you that you're going to mature as a Christian believer this year. Let this be a reminder to stay committed to complete the journey you've started to become a fully devoted follower of Christ.

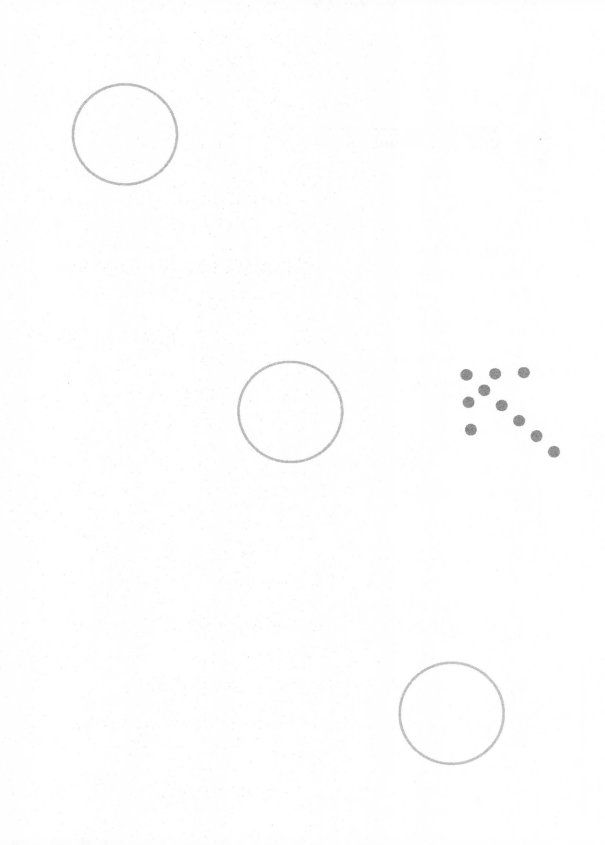

Devotion Four

d4   A Walk with God

Good job! You are on your way to learning more about becoming a fully devoted follower of Christ. Time alone with God is a key discipline in your spiritual journey. *It will change your life.* Just like finding time to talk on the phone or online strengthens a friendship, spending time with God is no different. Stay with it. It will make a difference in your life, and you will find out just how awesome a friendship with God can be.

see FOR YOURSELF

Highlight or underline these verses in your Bible:

>> **proverbs 18:24**
There are "friends" who destroy each other, but a real friend sticks closer than a brother.

>> **exodus 33:11**
Inside the Tent of Meeting, the LORD would speak to Moses face to face, as a man speaks to his friend.

ask YOURSELF

1. What do these passages say about God's friendship with you?

2. What do you think it was like for Moses to hear God speak to him "as a man speaks to his friend"?

3. Can you become a fully devoted follower without spending time with God or reading his Word? How does your view of spending time with God and reading his Word

change when you see them as getting to know God as your friend, rather than following a bunch of rules?

4. Think of the best positive experience you have ever had with friends. What made this experience so meaningful? How can your friendship with God have those same qualities?

think FOR YOURSELF

Think of all the names you know for God—for example, King, Lord, Savior, Almighty, the Great "I Am." Now add one more name to the list: *Friend*. How does knowing God as *friend* change your relationship with him, change your conversations with him? In the space below, write a letter to God as your friend, telling him you want to strengthen your friendship by spending each day in these Daily Devotions. Let him know your desire to build a lifelong friendship with him.

experience IT YOURSELF

In the space below, write out this phrase: "Fully Devoted Follower." Underneath, write "Fully Devoted Friend." Take some time now to talk to God just like you would any other friend. Let him know again your desire to build a friendship with him. Tell God you are looking forward to these devotion times with him in the coming weeks.

Devotion Five

d 5   **Be Yourself**

This study and devotion process will take you down an exciting path of spiritual adventure. It's very important that you are honest about who you are. Being yourself and honestly evaluating your relationship with God is one way for you to mature as a Christ-follower.

see FOR YOURSELF

Highlight or underline these verses in your Bible:

>> **psalm 119:11**
I have hidden your word in my heart, that I might not sin against you.

>> **1 timothy 4:16**
Keep a close watch on yourself and on your teaching. Stay true to what is right, and God will save you and those who hear you.

>> **romans 4:20–21**
Abraham never wavered *in believing God's promise.* In fact, his faith grew stronger, and in this he brought glory to God. *He was absolutely convinced* that God was able to do anything he promised.

ask YOURSELF

1. According to the first two passages, why is it important to know God's Word?

2. How sure are you when it comes to being "absolutely convinced" that God has the power to do what he has promised?

As a Christ-follower, how confident are you when it comes to knowing what you believe? On the continuum below, mark honestly where you are at this time in your journey with Christ. Let this be a starting point for where you want to see improvement during the coming weeks. Honestly evaluate yourself now by placing an X over the number on each continuum below that best describes where you are spiritually.

What I believe

1	2	3	4	5	6	7	8	9	10

I do not know what my faith believes — I know some of the basics of my faith — I know some, but am not confident about what I know — I feel confident about the truth of my faith

The Word of God

1	2	3	4	5	6	7	8	9	10

I do not know the Word of God — I know some stories in the Bible — I know the Word, and have a desire to know much more — I love to read God's Word—it's what helps me stay strong as a Christian

God's promises to me

1	2	3	4	5	6	7	8	9	10

I do not know God's promises to me — I'm not sure why it's important to know — I know some of God's promises to me — I know and believe with all my heart what God has promised to me

experience IT YOURSELF

Take a moment and pray, asking God to help you build a stronger friendship with him. Thank him for the small group he's given you during this study, and ask him to use your time with them and time alone to help you along your journey of becoming a fully devoted follower. Now go back to the continuums above and circle the number on each that describes where you want to be at the end of the entire study. Let this be a goal for you to achieve during this time.

This week, share with your group where you placed yourself on the continuums and let them know your commitment and desire to build a stronger friendship with God in the coming weeks.

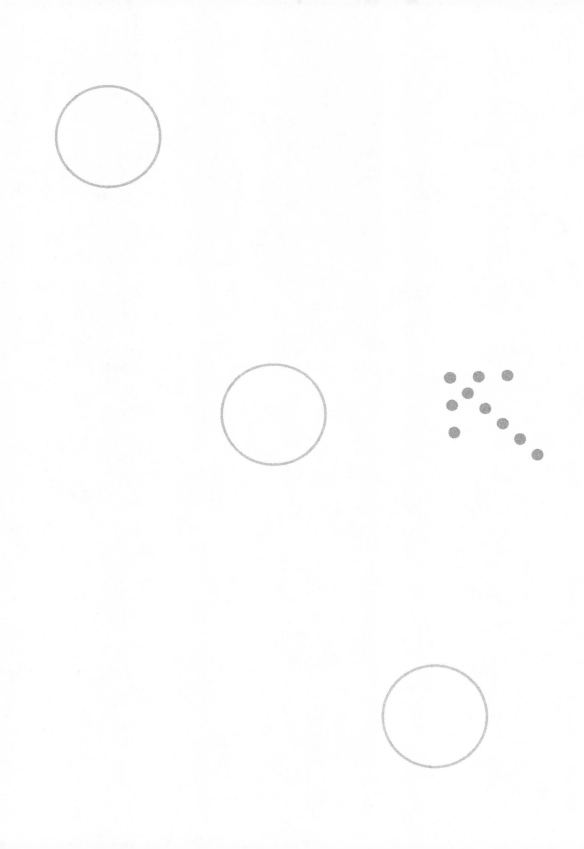

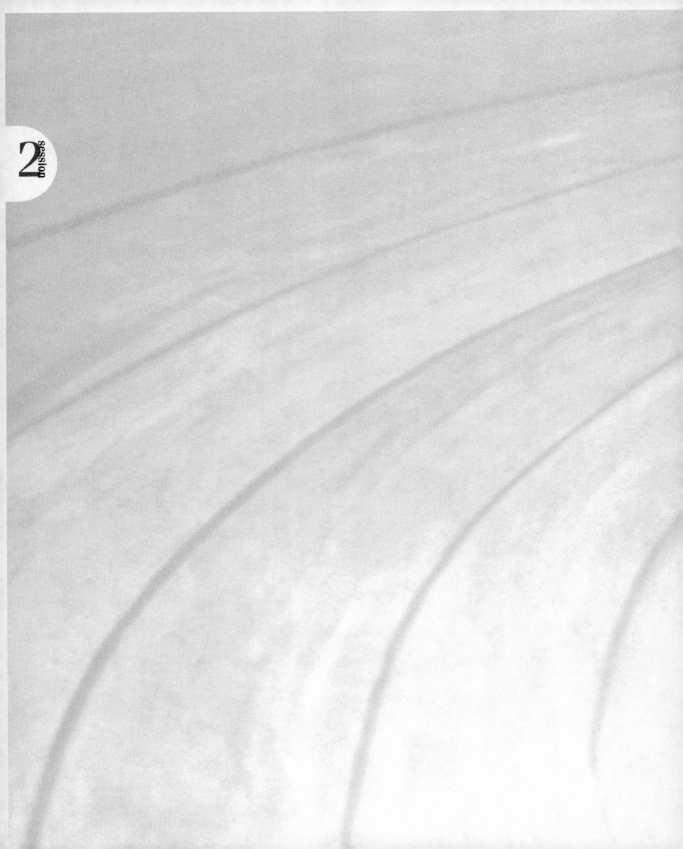

session
2

g² Grace

Part 1: A True Gift

week IN REVIEW

1. Describe for the rest of the group the richest insight you had from your Daily Devotions.

2. Describe the most meaningful activity you did.

3. Share where you placed yourself on the continuums on page 33.

4. What questions or concerns were raised by your Daily Devotions?

opening UP

In his book *What's So Amazing About Grace?* Philip Yancey tells the story of a girl from Traverse City, Michigan, who has problems relating to her parents. Her parents object to her nose ring, her music, her clothes—to the point where she feels the only solution is to run away. After making her way to Detroit, she meets a man who drives the fanciest car she has ever seen. He teaches her how to please men and puts her up in a penthouse apartment and dresses her in expensive clothes. For a year she lives the life of a high roller, selling her services while high on drugs. Then she begins to get sick. Her "boss" quickly turns her out and she soon finds herself living on the streets. Her cough worsens and she realizes she will not survive long living like this. Then she has an idea: *home.*

She calls her parents but only gets the answering machine. She devises a plan and leaves a message: "Dad, Mom, it's me. I was wondering about maybe coming home. I'm catching a bus up your way, and it'll get there about midnight tomorrow. If you're not there, well, I guess I'll just stay on the bus until it hits Canada." On the way she realizes that this was not a good plan. What if they were away and don't get the message? As the bus turns into the station in Traverse City at midnight, the driver says everyone has fifteen minutes before they have to be back on the bus. She doesn't know what to expect, but as she enters the terminal she sees something totally unexpected. About fifty of her relatives are there: brothers, sisters, cousins, aunts, uncles, grandmother, and great-grandmother— and her parents. They all have party hats and are standing under a huge banner that reads "Welcome Home."

That is grace, an unexpected gift, and in many ways it lies at the heart of the Christian life. *Grace* describes the fundamental basis of our relationship with God. Basically, it means "unearned gift" or "special favor." Through Jesus' death on the cross, we have received a special favor: the unearned gift of salvation.

1. Share a story about when you received grace from someone. (For example, you were speeding but you didn't get a ticket, or you received a gift you didn't deserve.)

2. How did receiving grace make you feel? Did it change the way you made decisions? Why or why not?

read TOGETHER

Read Jesus' story of the father with two sons.

>> luke 15:11–19

A man had two sons. The younger son told his father, "I want my share of your estate now, instead of waiting until you die." So his father agreed to divide his wealth between his sons.

A few days later this younger son packed all his belongings and took a trip to a distant land, and there he wasted all his money on wild living. About the time his money ran out, a great famine swept over the land, and he began to starve. He persuaded a local farmer to hire him to feed his pigs. The boy became so hungry that even the pods he was feeding the pigs looked good to him. But no one gave him anything.

When he finally came to his senses, he said to himself, "At home even the hired men have food enough to spare, and here I am, dying of hunger! I will go home to my father and say, 'Father, I have sinned against both heaven and you, and I am no longer worthy of being called your son. Please take me on as a hired man.'"

explore TOGETHER

1. Why do you think the father did as his son requested and gave him half his wealth?

2. What does it mean when it says, "the son finally came to his senses"? Has this ever happened to you, where you came to your senses about a certain situation? Explain.

3. After the son "came to his senses" and planned to return to his home, what did he expect from his father? Why?

read TOGETHER

Read Luke 15:20–24.

explore TOGETHER

1. What did the father think of his son's confession? What did the father do before the son spoke and what did he do after?

>> **luke 15:20–24**

So he returned home to his father. And while he was still a long distance away, his father saw him coming. Filled with love and compassion, he ran to his son, embraced him, and kissed him. His son said to him, "Father, I have sinned against both heaven and you, and I am no longer worthy of being called your son."

But his father said to his servants, "Quick! Bring the finest robe in the house and put it on him. Get a ring for his finger, and sandals for his feet. And kill the calf we have been fattening in the pen. We must celebrate with a feast, for this son of mine was dead and has now returned to life. He was lost, but now he is found." So the party began.

2. How was grace shown by the father to his son?

read TOGETHER

Read Luke 15:25–32.

>> **luke 15:25–32**

Meanwhile, the older son was in the fields working. When he returned home, he heard music and dancing in the house, and he asked one of the servants what was going on. "Your brother is back," he was told, "and your father has killed the calf we were fattening and has prepared a great feast. We are celebrating because of his safe return."

The older brother was angry and wouldn't go in. His father came out and begged him, but he replied, "All these years I've worked hard for you and never once refused to do a single thing you . . .
(cont.)

... told me to. And in all that time you never gave me even one young goat for a feast with my friends. Yet when this son of yours comes back after squandering your money on prostitutes, you celebrate by killing the finest calf we have."

His father said to him, "Look, dear son, you and I are very close, and everything I have is yours. We had to celebrate this happy day. For your brother was dead and has come back to life! He was lost, but now he is found!"

explore TOGETHER

1. Why was the older brother angry? Was his feeling justified?

2. Jesus told this story to show what our heavenly Father is like and to give us a picture of his grace. Look back on every action the father took. What do we learn about God our Father? What does that mean about what he is willing to do for you?

experience IT TOGETHER

Write down on a white board or flip chart the different names you can think of for *father* (for example, Daddy, Opo, Abba, Papa). After writing out the list, go around and pick one name you want to use and say, "God, you are my _____."
Then take turns saying it out loud. Let this be a reminder that God really is your heavenly Father who loves you and is always there for you.

community TIME

In prayer together, thank God for his gift of grace, that he is your heavenly Father, and for what you have learned in the study. Ask God to deepen your understanding of grace this week through the Daily Devotions.

Session 2

SESSION TWO

S² Grace

Part 1: A True Gift

In these Daily Devotions we will learn more about the true gift of God's grace, the first of the Five Gs. Keep track of questions or concerns you may have that you can ask about at the next Group Study time.

Devotion One

d 1

Accepting the Gift

Why go on a spiritual journey? Journeys take work: preparing, training, facing obstacles, perhaps even dangers. We do it because it is where we connect with God, and where we find forgiveness, freedom, and the purpose of life. Jesus, the Son of God, made this journey possible by giving his life for us on the cross. Only by Jesus dying and coming back to life can we hope to be reconnected to God and live the life we were meant to live—a life of forgiveness, joy, and adventure—where we learn to become more and more like Jesus. That journey begins when we accept what Jesus has done for us and receive the gift he wants to give us. This key concept is often described in the Bible as *grace,* which means "getting something we don't deserve or haven't earned."

see FOR YOURSELF

Highlight or underline these verses from the apostle Paul's letters in your Bible:

ask YOURSELF

1. Why is it important to Paul that we understand that grace is completely free—we cannot work for it or deserve it?

> **>> ephesians 2:8–10**
> God saved you by his special favor [grace] when you believed. And you can't take credit for this; it is a gift from God. *Salvation is not a reward for the good things we have done, so none of us can boast about it.* For we are God's masterpiece. He has created us anew in Christ Jesus.
>
> **>> romans 3:25**
> For God sent Jesus to take the punishment for our sins and to satisfy God's anger against us. *We are made right with God when we believe that Jesus shed his blood, sacrificing his life for us.*
>
> **>> romans 6:23**
> For the wages of sin is death, but *the free gift [grace] of God is eternal life through Christ Jesus our Lord.*

2. What role does Jesus play in our receiving this gift?

3. If it were not for Jesus, what fate do we deserve and why?

God's love and forgiveness are given to you not based on your performance or by successfully following rules you have to live by. They are completely free and received by faith in Jesus. In the space below, take a moment and thank him for this gift if you have received God's grace. If you have not accepted this gift of grace, think about and write down what is keeping you from taking the next step if you know what that is. Ask God to help you find the answers to the questions you have.

Light a candle in your room representing God's light and truth that he has provided for you to follow during your lifelong journey. Reread aloud the verses from page 44—and Ephesians 2:8–10, Romans 3:25; 6:23. Tell God how grateful you are that your sins* are forgiven, that you have a Father in heaven who is with you this day and promises to walk beside you the rest of your life. If you have not accepted Jesus' free gift of grace yet, reflect on what's holding you back.

---

*A *sin* is anything in thought, word, or deed that falls short of God's holy standards for us.

Devotion Two

A Gift of Freedom

Becoming a follower of Jesus means accepting the truth of who God is and what Jesus has done for us. But it also means accepting the truths about ourselves—especially the hard-to-admit ones that we don't want to think of ourselves, let alone feel willing to tell others. This is not the way God wants us to live. He wants us to willingly admit the hard truth about ourselves so we can experience real freedom. The freedom comes from accepting that God our Father accepts us by grace and we no longer have to pretend to be "good enough" to receive love. The radical truth is that God is ready to receive us no matter what we have done or ever will do!

see FOR YOURSELF

Highlight or underline in your Bible these verses:

>> **psalm 51:10–12**
Create in me a clean heart, O God.
Renew a right spirit within me.
Do not banish me from your presence,
and don't take your Holy Spirit from me.
Restore to me again the joy of your salvation,
and make me willing to obey you.

>> **1 john 1:9**
If we confess our sins [*sin* is anything opposed to God in thought, word, or deed] *to him, he is faithful* and just to forgive us and to cleanse us from every wrong.

>> **2 corinthians 3:16–18**
Whenever anyone turns to the Lord, then the veil [a covering of the face] *is taken away.* Now the Lord is the Spirit, and wherever the Spirit of the Lord is, he gives freedom. And all of us have had that veil removed so that we can be mirrors that brightly reflect the glory of the Lord. And as the Spirit of the Lord works within us, we become more and more like him and reflect his glory even more.

1. What masks (veils) do you wear that keep you from becoming a mirror that reflects Jesus in your life?

2. According to these verses, describe what happens when we come before God and confess the hard truths of our sins about ourselves.

In the space below write about the different ways you feel you have to measure up in your world: with friends, at school, in sports, with your family.

Looking over your list, consider how God has accepted you merely by grace, no matter what you look like, who you are, or what you have done. How does knowing about God's grace and acceptance change how you see yourself and change how you would handle the pressure to "measure up" in these relationships? Write your thoughts in the space below.

Psalm 103:12 states, "As far as the east is from the west, so far has he removed our transgressions from us." On your computer list all the ways you have fallen short of God's glory in your life. Be as specific as possible. After you have written as much as you can, read it over carefully, ask God for his forgiveness, and thank him for his grace. Then delete the file. That is what God has done with your sins as well. Say a prayer of thanksgiving for God's loving grace. (If you don't have access to a computer, write your list on paper. When you are done, rip up the paper and throw it in the trash.)

Devotion Three

d3

Noticing the Gift

Living in grace requires a new way of seeing. God is at work every day showing his grace to us, if only we have the eyes to see it. Jesus was an expert at this kind of seeing. When he saw sparrows, he saw how God provided food and care for them. When he saw beautiful lilies, he saw how God dressed them. We must train ourselves to notice God's grace, seeing his hand in a beautiful day, a safe home, a good talk with a friend. In other words, we must train ourselves to notice the ways God provides for us that we usually take for granted. Noticing these gifts can be fun, seeing all the ways the Father takes care of us and shows us his love. We also have the opportunity to say "thank you" and to trust more in God's care, which is a big part of the freedom we enjoy as Christ-followers.

see FOR YOURSELF

Highlight or underline in your Bible these verses from Jesus' encouraging and comforting Sermon on the Mount, recorded in Matthew's gospel:

ask YOURSELF

1. According to Jesus, how active is God the Father in taking care of plants and animals?

>>
matthew 6:25–33

[Jesus speaking] "I tell you, don't worry about everyday life—whether you have enough food, drink, and clothes. Doesn't life consist of more than food and clothing? Look at the birds. They don't need to plant or harvest or put food in barns because your heavenly Father feeds them. And you are far more valuable to him than they are. Can all your worries add a single moment to your life? Of course not.

"And why worry about your clothes? Look at the lilies and how they grow. They don't work or make their clothing, yet Solomon in all his glory was not dressed as beautifully as they are. And if God cares so wonderfully for flowers that are here today and gone tomorrow, won't he more surely care for you? . . .

"Your heavenly Father already knows all your needs, and he will give you all you need from day to day."

2. Compared to plants and animals, how does God want to care for us?

3. Why is it so easy to forget or not notice that God takes care of us? What prevents us from noticing all that he does for us?

4. Why does understanding how active God is in caring for us give us confidence not to worry about our daily needs?

think FOR YOURSELF

Think for a moment of all the ways you notice that God cares for nature (food for animals to eat, rain and sun for the plants, etc.). Now think through the last twenty-four hours in your life, paying attention to how God provided for you, even in the most ordinary ways (for example, water to drink, a bed to sleep in, clothes and shoes to wear). Make a list in the space below of at least ten things you find today that you are grateful God has provided. Thank him for his grace that he offers you every day.

experience IT YOURSELF

Write "24/7" (twenty-four hours a day, seven days of the week—in other words, all the time) on the back of your hand and keep it there for one full day. Let this remind you to notice the small, ordinary ways that we take for granted how God is caring for us 24/7. All throughout the day, give him thanks for his amazing care for you.

Devotion Four

d4 Living with the Gift Every Day

You *can* experience new life in Jesus Christ and be set free to live without fear of not measuring up. You don't need to earn God's love and he is willing to give you everything you need, 24/7. But how do you let God's grace help you when you are tempted to do things that could hurt you and hinder your relationship with him?

see FOR YOURSELF

Highlight or underline in your Bible these verses from the letter to the Hebrews and from Paul's first letter to the church in the city of Corinth:

ask YOURSELF

1. According to these verses, how does God view the areas we struggle with?

>> **hebrews 4:14–16**
We have a great High Priest who has gone to heaven, Jesus the Son of God. Let us cling to him and never stop trusting him. *This High Priest of ours understands our weaknesses, for he faced all of the same temptations we do,* yet he did not sin. So let us come boldly to the throne of our gracious God. There we will receive his mercy [*mercy* means "compassionate treatment by someone who has power over you"], and we will find grace to help us when we need it.

>> **1 corinthians 10:13**
Remember that the temptations that come into your life are no different from what others experience. And God is faithful. *He will keep the temptation from becoming so strong that you can't stand up against it.* When you are tempted, he will show you a way out so that you will not give in to it.

2. What is God doing while we are being tempted?

3. How can *grace* ("special favor" or "an unearned gift") be something that helps us when we are tempted or give in to sin?

In the space below, reflect on how God understands you—your struggles and your temptations. How does knowing that God will give you the grace to overcome your struggles or forgive you when you sin change how you feel about yourself and what you can accomplish? Thank him again for his amazing gift of grace.

Think of a mature Christian you can trust (for example, your youth pastor, a mature Christian leader, or a good Christian friend who knows how to keep things in confidence). Today or tomorrow let them know what you are struggling with and let them know how they can pray for and support you. We often receive God's grace through others.

Devotion Five

d5   An Everlasting Gift

Do you get it? Do you understand how grace works? That it is a free gift that God gives you every day to help you and to show his everlasting love? Have you fully accepted grace by telling God your need for him to be the leader of your life, and asking him for forgiveness? God wants us to rest in his grace forever. He wants us to be free from always trying harder to impress him or others, from the masks we feel we need to put on. Nothing can separate you from God's grace. Jesus will always be there for you. If you have not received this gift yet, what is stopping you?

see FOR YOURSELF

Highlight or underline in your Bible these verses from Israel's King David, the prophet Jeremiah, and the apostle Paul:

ask YOURSELF

1. According to these verses (which were written hundreds of years apart), how does God feel about us?

>> **psalm 23:6**
Surely your goodness and unfailing love [grace] will pursue me all the days of my life, and *I will live in the house of the LORD forever.*

>> **jeremiah 31:3**
Long ago the LORD said to Israel: "I have loved you, my people, with an everlasting love. *With unfailing love I have drawn you to myself."*

>> **romans 8:38–39**
I am convinced that nothing can ever separate us from his love. Death can't, and life can't. The angels can't, and the demons can't. Our fears for today, our worries for tomorrow, and even the powers of hell can't keep God's love away. Whether we are high above the sky or in the deepest ocean, *nothing in all creation will ever be able to separate us from the love of God* that is revealed in Christ Jesus our Lord.

2. Why do you think he loves us so deeply?

3. How would we live our lives differently if we really were convinced that God's love and grace for us is everlasting?

think FOR YOURSELF

Read Romans 8:38–39 from page 52 out loud. Rewrite the verses in the space below, putting them into your own words. Ask yourself if you are convinced of these truths. Then sign your name at the bottom, signifying that you are convinced of and thankful for God's awesome and never-ending gift of grace.

experience IT YOURSELF

Write "P.S. I love you, forever" in the front and in the back of your Bible as a reminder of God's everlasting love for you. Say a prayer letting God know you are thankful for his love and amazing grace.

GROUP THREE

g₃

Grace

Part 2: Sharing the Gift

week IN REVIEW

1. Describe for the rest of the group the richest insight you had from your Daily Devotions.

2. Describe the most meaningful activity you did.

3. What new ways have you noticed God's grace in your everyday life?

4. What questions or concerns were raised by your Daily Devotions?

opening UP

I saw myself as a "good guy" whom people liked. I got good grades, experimented with what I considered "mild" drugs, and looked forward to parties where I could drink with friends. Then I met Katie. She seemed different, like she knew what she was doing with her life. We started talking a lot, and I found out she was a Christian. She told me her story. She explained how she had felt abandoned when in eighth grade her parents divorced. To her surprise all these Christians stepped in to take care of her and become surrogate parents for her. She said it was God telling her that he had not abandoned her.

Her story reminded me that I had prayed months earlier—halfheartedly, since I really didn't believe God existed—that God would show himself to me if he was there. I had felt a little lost and wondered if my life was supposed to have a point. Katie was like the tenth Christian I had met at school after never meeting any before that. After meeting a couple more Christians, I realized that God was answering my prayer. I became a Christian that summer.

When school began again in the fall, I saw an old friend who asked me what I did that summer. I told him, "I discovered God." After the shock, he was curious and wanted to hear more. So I told him my story. It seemed so natural. Six months later he became a Christian too.

—Mike, 18

In the last session we explored the amazing story of God's grace, how he accepts us just as we are, no matter what we have done or said in the past. God's story of how Jesus is reaching out to us is so amazing, in fact, that we can't keep it to ourselves. It is a gift to be shared. But don't worry; that doesn't mean you need to enroll in a course on becoming a professional evangelist. We just need to learn how to tell our story, which is what we will explore in this session.

1. What words come to mind—both positive and negative—when you hear the word *evangelist?* In addition to making your own list below, have someone write down the words the group comes up with on a flip chart or white board where everyone can see them. Write the negative words in one column and the positive words in another.

Negative   **Positive**

2. When you look at the negative words, how does this impact your desire to evangelize (which means telling others about Jesus)?

3. When you look at the positive words, how does this impact your desire to evangelize?

4. God has a one-word job description for being an evangelist: *you.* You don't have to become someone you don't want to, or try to be someone you'll never be. God wants you to be yourself. How does knowing that you can be yourself free you up to tell others about God?

read TOGETHER

Read 2 Timothy 1:5–8.

>> **2 timothy 1:5–8**

I know that you sincerely trust the Lord, for you have the faith of your mother, Eunice, and your grandmother, Lois. This is why I remind you to fan into flames the spiritual gift God gave you when I laid my hands on you. *For God has not given us a spirit of fear and timidity, but of power, love, and self-discipline.* So you must never be ashamed to tell others about our Lord.

discuss TOGETHER

1. Why do you think Paul felt he had to reassure Timothy?

2. Why should Paul's words encourage Timothy to talk to others about his relationship with Jesus?

3. How do you feel when you think about telling someone what Jesus has done in your life? How do Paul's words affect you?

In groups of two, give each other three minutes to share your story of how you met Christ. If you're not sure yet about your relationship with Christ, describe where you are now on your spiritual journey.

After telling your stories, share the name of a friend who is still seeking to understand God. Tell how you know them. Pray together for God to provide the right opportunity to talk to your friend about God.

Light a candle and think about the friend you want to come to know Jesus as Forgiver and Leader. Go around the group, one at a time, and say the name of your friend out loud and let the lit candle represent the hope that someday they will see the light. Close in prayer, thanking God in advance for what he is going to do in the lives of your friends.

SESSION THREE

S³

Grace

Part 2: Sharing the Gift

In the last session we explored the amazing story of God's grace, of how he takes care of us daily and saves us freely through Jesus. God desires for all to know his love. And what's exciting is that God wants to use you to share his love. In this session you'll learn how you can share God's grace with others.

Devotion One

d¹   **Being Real**

We've studied how God has offered the gift of becoming a Christ-follower freely—by grace. We do not need to earn it, only receive it. But grace does not end when Christ becomes our leader. The good news is that we also live and *minister* by grace. God is not looking for perfect disciples to do his work. He wants to use ordinary, real people—like you.

s e e FOR YOURSELF

Highlight or underline in your Bible these verses from the apostle Paul's letter to the Roman and Ephesian churches and from the apostle John's first letter:

>>
romans 10:12–14

All have the same Lord, who generously gives his riches to all who ask for them. For "Anyone who calls on the name of the Lord will be saved."

But how can they call on him to save them unless they believe in him? And how can they believe in him if they have never heard about him? And *how can they hear about him unless someone tells them?*

>> **1 john 1:3**

We are telling you about *what we ourselves have actually seen and heard,* so that you may have fellowship with us.

>> **ephesians 3:7–8**

By God's special favor [grace] *and mighty power,* I have been given the wonderful privilege of serving him by spreading this Good News.

a s k YOURSELF

1. In the verse from Romans above, Paul is wondering how to get the word out about what Jesus has done for us. What role might you play in your answer to Paul's questions?

2. Often we think it is up to the experts (pastors, leaders, youth ministers, full-time evangelists)—people who have studied Scripture and theology for many years—to talk to others about Jesus. But what is John saying about what he wants to tell those he is writing to?

3. God is working in your life every day. What have you "actually seen and heard" in your life with God that you can tell others about? Remember that your own story is a great testimony of how God is working.

4. According to Paul in Ephesians, whose favor and power works through Paul's efforts? What did Paul do to deserve this privilege?

think FOR YOURSELF

In the space below, write down the worries you have about talking to others about Jesus. Ask God to help you overcome your fears. Remember, you do not have to become someone you're not; you just need to be yourself. God wants to use you to share his love with the seeking friends in your life. Let God know that you're willing to overcome your fears to share his love with your friends.

experience IT YOURSELF

Start an Impact List. On this list, name three friends who are not Christ-followers. This will be a reminder for you to pray for them and to ask God to use you to help them along their spiritual journey. Tape this list on your bathroom mirror to remind you to pray for them each morning.

Devotion Two

d² You Have a Story

A wonderful story of sharing grace is told in John's gospel. Jesus sees a blind man in Jerusalem, kneels down besides him, spits on some dirt to make mud, and applies the mud to the man's blind eyes. Then he simply tells the man, "Go and wash in the pool." The man does and returns able to see. The crowds can't believe it. Some say it is not the same man, only someone who looks like him. The man assures them that he was the blind man. The Pharisees are upset that Jesus performed this miracle on the Sabbath, when no one is allowed to do any work. They interrogated the man and even ordered his parents in for questioning. The man stuck to what he knew: "I was blind, and now I can see!"

While we don't all have dramatic stories like his, we all have a wonderful story of how we came to Christ. God is active in every Christian's life. *How* God is active in our lives is what those seeking God need to hear.

see FOR YOURSELF

Highlight or underline in your Bible these verses from John's gospel:

>> **john 9:10 – 12, 24 – 25**

They asked, "Who healed you? What happened?"

He told them, "The man they call Jesus made mud and smoothed it over my eyes and told me, 'Go to the pool of Siloam and wash off the mud.' I went and washed, and now I can see!"

"Where is he now?" they asked.

"I don't know," he replied. . . .

So for the second time they called in the man who had been blind and told him, "Give glory to God by telling the truth, because we know Jesus is a sinner."

"I don't know whether he is a sinner," the man replied. "But I know this: I was blind, and now I can see!"

1. Why were the religious leaders upset with the man's story? Why was the man's testimony so powerful and so hard to refute?

2. What qualified the blind man to be a witness for Jesus?

3. Very few people have such dramatic stories as the blind man in John 9. But God is active in each and every one of his followers. What stories could you tell of how God has acted in your life or those around you?

4. Remember, every believer has an awesome story of how they came to know God as Forgiver and Leader. Do you believe this to be true about your own story? Why or why not?

think FOR YOURSELF

Thank God for your own story and the people God used to tell you about his love. Remember that your story is the time that God called you to himself. Think about that for a moment: The King of kings and Lord of lords knows you by name! It's awesome that God not only knows you but has chosen you to be the messenger of his love. Take some time now to remember your own story of how you became a Christ-follower. Think about the people that God used to teach you about his love. Now, in the space below (and on the next page), write down all the people that God used. Say a prayer of thankfulness for how God used these people in your life. Ask him to let you be a person who can be used in one of your friends' lives to share his love.

experience IT YOURSELF

Send an email or write a note to the people (or person) God used to help you become a Christ-follower. Thank them for what they did. This is a great way to encourage them and remind them that they are "difference-makers" and that God is pleased with them.

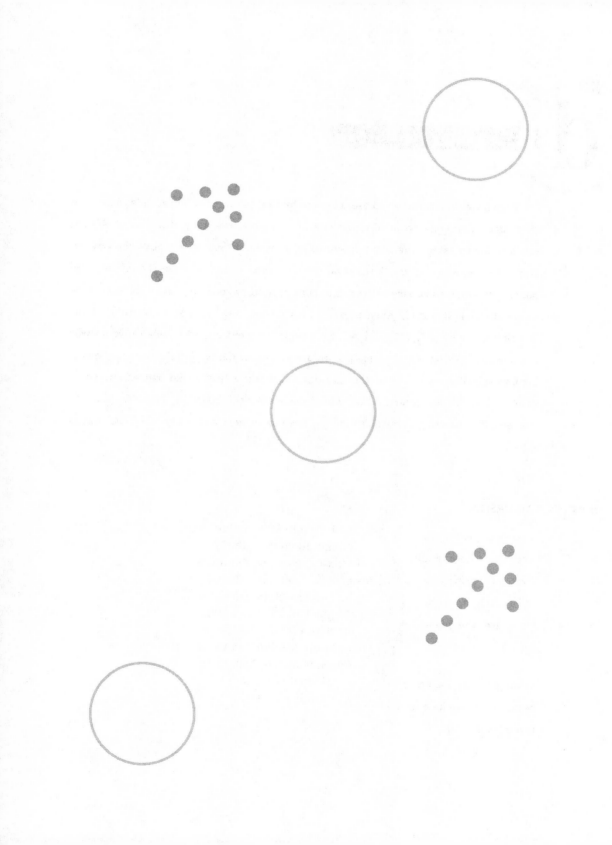

Devotion Three

d3 **Telling Your Story**

Which would you rather go see, a lecture by an economist who uses slides filled with many statistics on poverty in Africa or a movie telling the true story of two South African teens trying to escape the shantytowns of Johannesburg? Stories are powerful ways to communicate, which is why Jesus used them so often—and why we should too. The people you know and do life with want to hear your story because you are someone they can relate to. In this study you are going to learn how to tell your story by using a clear and simple outline: BC, MC, and AC. BC stands for "before Christ," where we answer the question, "What was your life like before you knew Christ?" MC stands for "meeting Christ," where we answer the question, "How did Christ make himself known to you?" AC stands for "after Christ," where we answer the question, "How has your life changed after meeting Christ?" You simply have to be clear and ready—like Paul was in Acts 26.

see FOR YOURSELF

There's a great story in Acts 26 where Paul gives his testimony before King Agrippa. Here are the highlights of the story.

In verses 4–11, Paul tells of his life before he encountered Jesus (BC):

BC
"...I used to believe that I ought to do everything I could to oppose the followers of Jesus of Nazareth.... Many times I had them whipped in the synagogues to try to get them to curse Christ. I was so violently opposed to them that I even hounded them in distant cities of foreign lands."

In verses 12–18, he explains how he met the Lord Jesus (MC):

MC

"A light from heaven brighter than the sun shone down on me and my companions. We all fell down, and I heard a voice saying to me in Aramaic, 'Saul, Saul, why are you persecuting me? It is hard for you to fight against my will.'

"'Who are you, sir?' I asked.

"And the Lord replied, 'I am Jesus, the one you are persecuting.'"

In verses 19–23, he concludes his testimony with what happened to him after the encounter (AC):

AC

"O King Agrippa, I was not disobedient to that vision from heaven. I preached first to those in Damascus, then in Jerusalem and throughout all Judea, and also to the Gentiles, that all must turn from their sins and turn to God—and prove they have changed by the good things they do."

a s k YOURSELF

1. Would you be able to tell your story to a seeking friend in a clear, simple way?

2. What would make it difficult for you to give your story of how you came to know Christ?

3. Why is it important for you to be ready to give a testimony of what God has done and is doing in your life?

(**think** FOR YOURSELF)

Practice writing out your story of how you met Jesus using the three parts mentioned above: BC, MC, then AC. Use an extra sheet of paper if you need to.

1. BC (Before Christ): What were you like before you came to Christ? What made you start thinking Christ could make a difference in your life?

   For example, "When I was in junior high my parents got divorced. I felt abandoned and angry. The last thing I wanted to do was trust God to lead my life."

   Note: If you became a Christian at a young age you might not have much of a BC history to talk about. That's okay. You can start with the next question.

2. MC (Meeting Christ): What was it that finally motivated you to trust in Christ? How did you receive Christ?

   For example, "I began to see that I didn't have complete control of my life and that the anger I felt wasn't solving any of my problems. During this time my best friend really stuck by my side and I saw how kind and different she was. I knew it was because she was a Christian. I began to wonder if Christ could make a difference in my life too.

   "When I asked my best friend about God, she told me that I mattered to God and that he wanted to help me. I knew then that I needed God and that only he could take away the anger in my heart.

   "My friend invited me to pray with her. I asked Christ to forgive me and be the leader of my life. I asked him to forgive my anger and all my other sins and then to help me forgive my parents."

3. AC (After Christ): How did your life begin to change after you came to Christ? What other benefits have you experienced since you became a Christian?

For example, "It was good to finally understand that God had forgiven me, that he would never abandon me, and that I could trust him. My life is no longer filled with anger.

"Knowing I am forgiven and loved by God helped me learn how to forgive and love my parents again and my relationship with them is much better. Whenever things get hard, I can read the Bible and get God's help and direction. I have a small group of Christian friends who encourage and support me and I know I'm going to spend eternity with God in heaven."

Note: If you became a Christian at a young age, compare your life now with what it might have been like if you had not come to Christ. *For example,* "I grew up in a Christian home and gave my life to Christ when I was pretty young. Even though I don't have a story about how my life used to be crazy without God, I know God has made a real difference in my life. I've had some problems and hard times and I've been able to rely on God during these times so I never felt alone. My faith has given me a lot of direction and understanding I wouldn't have otherwise."

experience IT YOURSELF

Using the BC, MC, AC method, practice telling your story this week to a Christian friend, family member, or small group leader. After you tell your story, ask if it was clear: Was the language something a non-Christian could understand? Remember to keep it short, about three to four minutes—something you could tell a friend at school during a break between classes. Remember that God wants to use you in your friends' lives. Now you will be ready when the time comes. Take time to pray now for those on your Impact List (see page 63), and ask God to provide the opportunity for you to tell your story.

Devotion Four

d 4   Growing in Compassion

We have studied how true spirituality is imitating Jesus and that Jesus was all about loving God and others. We share the gift of grace out of love for others. But sometimes sharing words and stories are not all God calls us to do in order to show his love.

see FOR YOURSELF

Highlight or underline in your Bible this story Jesus told as recorded in Luke's gospel:

>> **luke 10:30 – 37**

[Jesus speaking] "A Jewish man was traveling on a trip from Jerusalem to Jericho, and he was attacked by bandits. They stripped him of his clothes and money, beat him up, and left him half dead beside the road.

"By chance a Jewish priest came along; but when he saw the man lying there, he crossed to the other side of the road and passed him by. A Temple assistant walked over and looked at him lying there, but he also passed by on the other side.

"Then a despised Samaritan [a race of people 'good Jews' were forbidden to associate with] came along, and when he saw the man, he felt deep pity. Kneeling beside him, the Samaritan soothed his wounds with medicine and bandaged them. Then he put the man on his own donkey and took him to an inn, where he took care of him. The next day he handed the innkeeper two pieces of silver and told him to take care of the man. . . .

. . . 'If his bill runs higher than that,' he said, 'I'll pay the difference the next time I am here.'

"Now which of these three would you say was a neighbor to the man who was attacked by bandits?" Jesus asked.

The man replied, "The one who showed him mercy."

Then Jesus said, "Yes, *now go and do the same.*"

1. What was different about the third traveler compared to the first two?

2. Jesus told this story to explain the command "to love your neighbor as yourself" and in response to the question, "Who is my neighbor?" According to the story, who is and who is not your neighbor?

think FOR YOURSELF

In Matthew 9:36, we see Jesus' heart for people: "When he saw the crowds, he had compassion on them, because they were harassed and helpless, like sheep without a shepherd" (TNIV). As we become more like Jesus, we need to see others as Jesus sees them.

In the space below, write down at least three ways you could develop your compassion for others at your school who are not Christ-followers. For example, you could pray for them, give words of encouragement, be kind, avoid judging, etc. Ask God to give you opportunities this week to show compassion to others—to be an example of his love in both words and actions.

experience IT YOURSELF

Put a Band-Aid on your hand and wear it to school. Remind yourself every time you look at the Band-Aid of how God is meeting your needs and how he wants you to have compassion to meet the needs of others around you. Look for opportunities throughout the day to help others. Ask God to let you see people the way he sees them, remembering that people matter to God.

Devotion Five

d5   One Life at a Time

My junior year, I really wanted to make a big difference in the world. The only thing was, I wasn't sure what I was supposed to do. One day, as I discussed this with my small group leader, she pointed out that all I had to do was make a difference in one person's life at a time.

—Jessica, 15

s e e FOR YOURSELF

Highlight or underline in your Bible these verses from Luke's gospel:

a s k YOURSELF

>> luke 15:8 – 10
[Jesus speaking] "Suppose a woman has ten valuable silver coins and loses one. Won't she light a lamp and look in every corner of the house and sweep every nook and cranny until she finds it? And when she finds it, she will call in her friends and neighbors to rejoice with her because she has found her lost coin. *In the same way, there is joy in the presence of God's angels when even one sinner repents.*"

1. In this story, Jesus explains to the religious leaders why he is spending time with those sinners who were shunned by all good people: What did he want them to understand?

2. How does God view those who do not know him? What is he prepared to do to reach them?

3. Jesus makes three points in the passage on page 74: (1) something valuable was lost, (2) there was an all-out search, and (3) there was a celebration in the end. How is this a model for sharing our faith with others? How is this an inside look at how God sees lost people?

think FOR YOURSELF

How does God want to use you, one life at a time? Take a moment and look back at your Impact List (see page 63). Pick one friend in whose life you want God to use you to show his love. Be committed to pray for this friend throughout the year. Be willing to share your story and God's story. Build a friendship; it's more than just looking at your friend as an object to "win over." It's about really being a friend who will listen and be sensitive to them. Remember too that coming to Christ is a process—more like a marathon than a sprint. Be patient.

In the space below, write down your friend's name, then write a prayer asking God to use you to help your friend come to know Christ as the Leader and Forgiver of their life. Ask God to answer your prayer this year, thanking him in advance for what he is going to do.

experience IT YOURSELF

Write down your friend's name on an index card and place the card in your Bible next to John 3:16 ("For God so loved the world that he gave his only Son, so that everyone who believes in him will not perish but have eternal life"). This is to remind you that God loves your friend and that you need to be ready to be used by God to make an eternal difference in your friend's life this year.

session

4

g₄ Growth

GROUP FOUR

Part 1: Loving God

1. Describe for the rest of the group the richest insight you had from your Daily Devotions.

2. Describe the most meaningful activity you did.

3. What friend's name did you put in your Bible?

4. What questions or concerns were raised by your Daily Devotions?

opening UP

My brothers were the jocks in my family. They played baseball, basketball, and soccer, and summers were filled with sports camps. I spent my time hanging out with friends from school and my church group. In ninth grade some of them decided to try cross-country running. Since I wanted to be with them, I signed up. My dad couldn't believe it. The early practices were awful. I got sweaty, red in the face, and sore. One girl threw up during practice! I wanted to quit, but my dad told me it would get easier once I got into shape—plus he wouldn't let me quit. I got mad and told him I was already "in shape," but he ignored me.

After a couple of weeks, I noticed I wasn't as sore after running. Then my times started to get better. After a few weeks, I started to finish with the fastest runners. By the end of the season, I was winning some races. I remember my dad's shock when my coach told him I was a "natural" athlete and the team's "star." I was shocked too. I always thought I stunk at sports. I never would have known I was a natural runner unless I had started practicing every day after school.

—Katie, 16

Almost every area of our lives requires training if we want to do something well. Even friendships. We cannot really be a good friend until we have spent time together doing those activities that allow us to get to know each other. The same is true with knowing God better and being transformed to be more and more like Jesus. It doesn't just happen—*presto-chango, you are transformed!* It requires that we spend time doing those activities that allow us to get to know God better. We call these activities "spiritual disciplines," and we will explore how these work this week.

1. If you had to run a marathon tomorrow, what would happen? Why?

2. If you had six months to train to run the marathon, would it make a difference? Why?

3. Training gets us in condition to do things we are not fit to do right now, even if we try really hard. If we're not in condition, we won't get the results we're looking for. We simply are not ready to perform, so we must train. What have you trained for that made you able to do something that you were unable to do before (such as playing music, reciting a poem, performing in a play, playing a sport)? What effect did training and practice have?

>> **1 corinthians 9:25–27**

All athletes practice strict self-control. They do it to win a prize that will fade away, but we do it for an eternal prize. So I run straight to the goal with purpose in every step. I am not like a boxer who misses his punches. I discipline my body like an athlete, training it to do what it should. Otherwise, I fear that after preaching to others I myself might be disqualified.

read TOGETHER

Read aloud this passage from Paul's letter to the church in Corinth:

discuss TOGETHER

1. What did Paul fear would happen if he did not undergo a training discipline?

2. In a race, an athlete gets disqualified when he or she breaks a rule of the competition. Since Paul is one of the premier teachers of grace, what do you think Paul could mean by "disqualified"? How could you be "disqualified" in your ministry to your friends?

3. How would someone get back into racing after being disqualified? How would someone get back into the spiritual race after being disqualified? Keep in mind what we
learned in the last session about God's grace.

community TIME

What training activities—often called spiritual disciplines—do you need in your life right
now and why? For example, times of solitude, prayer, or serving others.

In prayer together, thank God for the opportunities we have for getting to know him better and learning to love him more. Also, ask God to help you "see" the many spontaneous
training opportunities you have each day to learn to be more like Jesus.

experience IT TOGETHER

Pair off with your accountability partner. Share what spiritual discipline you will work on
this week and exactly what you will do. Exchange email addresses and phone numbers
and pick a time to email or call each other for encouragement.

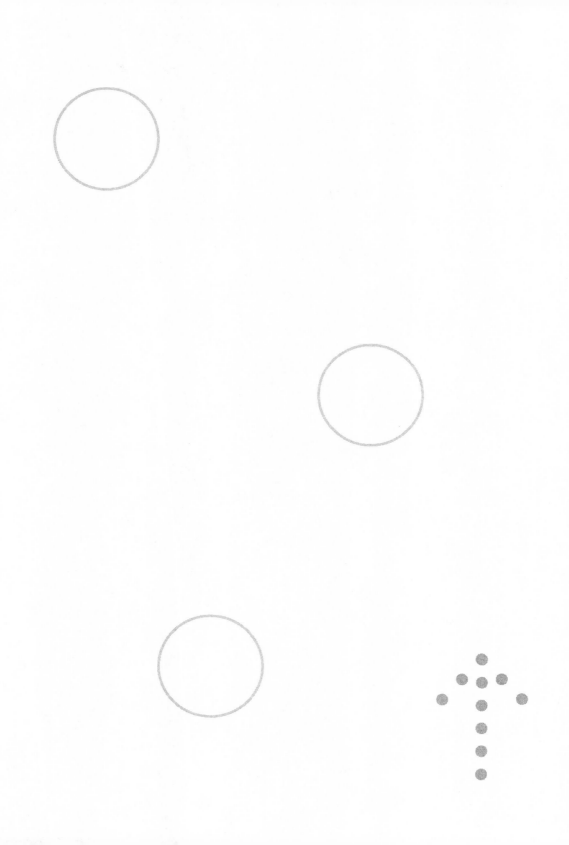

session

4

S⁴ Growth

Part 1: Loving God

In this session we will explore spiritual disciplines because we want to learn about Growth. Being a Christian should be synonymous with "becoming more like Jesus." God expects us always to be growing as we become more and more like his Son. The best measure of our growth is whether we are becoming more loving. In this session week we will look at how we deepen our love relationship with God—by using the spiritual disciplines that allow us to know, hear, and see God more clearly.

Devotion One

d 1   Training Smarter vs. Harder

My sophomore year, I transferred to a Christian school. I felt that by learning about the Bible and church history in school, I would be able to develop my faith more. A few weeks into school I couldn't believe how lucky I was to be around strong Christians and to study the Word of God in school! As I walked out of class one day, a friend asked what I was doing that weekend. She invited me to a party and said that it was going to be tons of fun since her parents were going to be out of town. She said, "My older sister is even buying beer for us, and Steve is bringing some pot." I couldn't believe it; she had just prayed out loud in our class, and now she was saying this? It took me awhile to sort all of this out, but I finally learned that Christian rules don't always make a difference in a person's life. What matters is how people relate to Jesus on a personal level, in their everyday life. Just going to a Christian school didn't make me more spiritual; it is what I let God do with my life each day that makes a difference.

—*Christine, 15*

see FOR YOURSELF

Highlight or underline these verses in your Bible:

>> **mark 1:35 – 37**
The next morning Jesus awoke long before daybreak and *went out alone into the wilderness to pray.* Later Simon and the others went out to find him. They said, "Everyone is asking for you."

>> **luke 6:12**
One day soon afterward Jesus went to a mountain to pray, and *he prayed to God all night.*

>> **romans**
12:1–2

Dear brothers and sisters, I plead with you to give your bodies to God. Let them be a living and holy sacrifice—the kind he will accept. When you think of what he has done for you, is this too much to ask? *Don't copy the behavior and customs of this world, but let God transform you into a new person by changing the way you think.* Then you will know what God wants you to do, and you will know how good and pleasing and perfect his will really is.

1. Think about how busy Jesus was ministering to people's needs. What did he have to do to spend time with God? What do you do to spend time alone with God?

2. How do we avoid copying "the behavior and customs of this world"? What do you think it means to offer our bodies to God as "a living and holy sacrifice"? What are some ways we can change how we think?

3. What activities or disciplines do you do that encourage or train you to become more like Jesus? Which disciplines would you like to add to help you train to be more like Jesus?

think FOR YOURSELF

Review your day as if you were watching it on video. Think through each part of the day and identify two or three instances you could have used as training opportunities for becoming more like Jesus. For instance, your car wouldn't start or your ride was late picking you up and so you ask yourself, "How can this moment train me in patience?" Or you're at school and someone says hurtful words; ask yourself, "How can this moment train me in self-control and love?" Or you have an assignment due in school tomorrow, but you find yourself online procrastinating. Ask yourself, "How can this teach me perseverance and self-control?" If you were complaining about homework or what your parents demanded of you, ask yourself, "How could this moment train me in gratitude for all God has given me instead of train me in ingratitude by focusing only on how hard I think my life is?" Perhaps you could have stopped before responding and tried to imagine more fully why your teacher or parents made a demand of you. Remember, all of life is a training ground for becoming more like Jesus.

experience IT YOURSELF

Look for training moments tomorrow at school. See how many opportunities you have to be more like Jesus in everyday actions. Ask God to help you see opportunities to become more like him.

Devotion Two

d²

"Be Silent, and Know That I Am God!"

I really want to make God a priority in my life. My small group leader says I can do this by spending some quiet time with God each day. But I just can't seem to find the time. I am always rushing off to school, without even enough time for breakfast. Then the school day goes by in a blur and all of a sudden I am off to practice or work or studies. I feel like it's all I can do to make it through the day, let alone have enough time with God. Do other people feel this way too?

—Janie, 17

see FOR YOURSELF

Highlight or underline in your Bible this verse from the Psalms:

>> **psalm 46:10**
"Be silent, and know that I am God!"

ask YOURSELF

1. Why do you think God wants us to be "silent" or "still" first before we meditate [think about or reflect on intentionally] on his presence? How does being still help us to know that God is God?

2. Where in your life do you experience silence or stillness?

3. What activities or practices do you do that demonstrate that you *know* that God is God? For instance, do you pray regularly? Do you take walks that allow you to meditate on God?

Set aside fifteen minutes to be completely quiet. Ask others in the house not to disturb you and make sure the phone or TV cannot intrude. Before you begin by following the guidelines below, here are a few things to keep in mind. The point of taking the time to be silent is to give your soul the space it needs to be aware of your life and of what God is doing in it. You don't have to manufacture a profound experience. All you have to do is show up and listen—God does the rest. Don't worry if you get distracted or feel like you don't hear anything. God is delighted simply because you come and want to spend time with him. It's not any more complicated than that.

1 *Find a quiet place.* Light a candle as a symbol of God's presence with you and set it nearby.

2 *Quiet your mind.* To help you do this, have a pen and notebook nearby to jot down any anxious thoughts that come to mind about how busy you are or things you need to do. Write them down so you can clear your mind, knowing you can come back to your notes later. Take a few deep breaths and relax.

3 *Be silent.* Listen to what God has to say to you. You may recall a moment in your day you could have handled better, or one that was handled particularly well. A person may come to your mind you want to pray for.

4 *Close with prayer.* End your time of listening by quietly speaking a prayer of thanks. For example, "Thank you, God, for being with me right now."

When we are truly still and silent—when our thoughts get quiet as well as our bodies—then we have created a space to see the big picture. In the space below, write down any impressions or thoughts you had while you were being silent. How hard was it to be silent? Do you think God was trying to tell you something? If so, what was it?

Devotion Three

d³ A Breath Prayer

Have you ever caught yourself muttering something under your breath? You might have been frustrated or angry, or maybe even trying to remember something in the busyness of your day. What would happen if prayer became so real to you that you really believed Jesus is always beside you, trying to hear what you were muttering? What would it take for you to direct those needs, frustrations, or questions to God?

see FOR YOURSELF

Highlight or underline these verses from the apostle Paul and from Jesus in Matthew's gospel:

>> **1 thessalonians 5:16–18** (NKJV)
Rejoice always, pray without ceasing, in everything give thanks; for this is the will of God in Christ Jesus for you.

>> **matthew 6:5–8**
[Jesus speaking] "When you pray, don't be like the hypocrites who love to pray publicly on street corners and in the synagogues where everyone can see them. I assure you, that is all the reward they will ever get. But when you pray, go away by yourself, shut the door behind you, and pray to your Father secretly. Then your Father, who knows all secrets, will reward you.

"When you pray, don't babble on and on as people of other religions do. They think their prayers are answered only by repeating their words again and again. Don't be like them, because your Father knows exactly what you need even before you ask him!"

1. According to Jesus in Matthew 6:5–8, what are two ways we should be cautious of praying? What do you think was the real motive behind the prayers of the people Jesus described as hypocrites?

2. In contrast to the wrong motives, what does Jesus advise us to do when we want to pray to God? Why do you think these are the prayers the Father wants to hear?

3. How does God's role change in answering prayers when we offer them with a humble and sincere heart?

think FOR YOURSELF

Breath prayers can be used to help with reading the Bible. It's known as "Bible meditation." After reading God's Word, you can take time to pray breath prayers—short little prayers asking God to support you, to lead you, and to help you apply what you just read. Let's try it with each phrase of Psalm 139:23–24. For example, after the first phrase, "Search me, O God, and know my heart," you might tell God what's on your heart by praying, "God, please help me; my heart is so sad lately." Now go ahead and try it.

> Search me, O God, and know my heart;
>
> test me and know my thoughts.
>
> Point out anything in me that offends you,
>
> and lead me along the path of everlasting life.

Thank God that he wants to hear from you at any time of the day. Thank him that he's there for you, and you can depend on him.

experience IT YOURSELF

We do not need a special occasion or a special place in order to talk with God. We can say a quick prayer anywhere at any time. These "breath prayers" are short, thought-prayers you say in whatever circumstances you're in. For example, you might:

Ask God for something: "Lord, help me get this homework done; I am so tired."

Thank God for something: "Thank you for getting me through that difficult conversation. You really take care of me."

Keep the communication lines open: "God, I'm feeling down today."

Tomorrow, practice saying breath prayers throughout the day. These prayers will help you to remember you are not alone—God is always with you.

Devotion Four

d4   **Bible Meditation**

Have you ever liked a song so much that you opened the CD case to read all the words in the liner notes? Then you played the song over and over again, singing along until you knew the whole thing by heart? You might not like to admit you were singing to yourself in the car or in your room, but most of us have done it! We liked the song so much we wanted to be able to participate in it, to know all of the words because they meant something to us, or touched a part of our hearts in ways that we weren't able to express before. God intends the Bible to be like this for us, to be even more meaningful than a favorite song, and to help us understand his love for us and the purpose he has for our lives.

see FOR YOURSELF

Highlight or underline these verses from the apostle Paul's letters to his young apprentice Timothy and to the church at Rome:

ask YOURSELF

1. What are all the uses of Scripture Paul lists in 2 Timothy 3:15–17? Underline each one.

>>
2 timothy 3:15 – 17
You have been taught the holy Scriptures from childhood, and they have given you the wisdom to receive the salvation that comes by trusting in Christ Jesus. *All Scripture is inspired by God and is useful to teach us* what is true and to make us realize what is wrong in our lives. It straightens us out and teaches us to do what is right. It is God's way of preparing us in every way, fully equipped for every good thing God wants us to do.

>> **romans 12:2**
Don't copy the behavior and customs of this world, but *let God transform you into a new person by changing the way you think.* Then you will know what God wants you to do, and you will know how good and pleasing and perfect his will really is.

2. Paul warns us not to be shaped by "the behavior and customs of this world" but to be transformed into a new person "by changing the way you think." How does meditation on Scripture transform us and change our thinking?

3. How do you think the Bible equips us "for every good thing God wants us to do"?

We are going to practice praying the Scriptures. After each phrase of Psalm 23, write a one-line prayer expressing how each phrase applies to you.

For example: *The LORD is my shepherd; I have everything I need.*

  God, thank you for watching over me and providing what I need.

  The LORD is my shepherd; I have everything I need.

  He lets me rest in green meadows; he leads me beside peaceful streams.

  He renews my strength. He guides me along right paths, bringing honor to his name.

Even when I walk through the dark valley of death, I will not be afraid, for you are close beside me.

Your rod and your staff protect and comfort me.

You prepare a feast for me in the presence of my enemies. You welcome me as a guest, anointing my head with oil. My cup overflows with blessings.

Surely your goodness and unfailing love will pursue me all the days of my life, and I will live in the house of the LORD forever.

experience IT YOURSELF

Before you go to sleep tonight, choose one verse from Psalm 23 above and meditate on it—which means saying it over and over again, thinking about each word and how you can apply it to your life. Try to keep this verse in your thoughts throughout the next day. Be aware of how the verse can be applied to the events of your day.

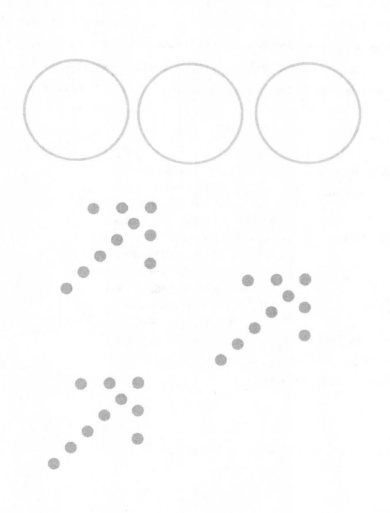

Devotion Five

d 5   Dream Big

One of the hardest truths for people to believe is that the Creator of the universe cares about the details of their lives. How can a God who tracks the paths of galaxies care about a person whose main concern is how a friend is not being as nice as he or she once was. But that is what God has told us. He knows even the number of hairs on your head (Matthew 10:30). And what is still more amazing, he has a plan for your life!

see FOR YOURSELF

Highlight or underline in your Bible these verses from the Old Testament:

>> **jeremiah 29:11 – 14**

"For *I know the plans I have for you*," says the LORD. "They are plans for good and not for disaster, to give you a future and a hope. In those days when you pray, I will listen. If you look for me in earnest, you will find me when you seek me. I will be found by you," says the LORD.

ask YOURSELF

1. How does this encourage you that God can deliver on his promise?

2. What is God promising to you in this passage?

3. What do you think God's plan for you is?

Take a moment and tell God how thankful you are for his plan for your life—even if you aren't yet sure what it is. Think through how your life has unfolded so far and how God has worked in it. Think about the following questions and use them to help you write a "God dream" for your life in the space below. What passions and desires has God given you? Now think about the future. How might you use those passions to serve God five years from now? What ministry might you be involved in? What difference might you make in the world with God's help? Think about how lives will be changed and how your generation can bring change to the world. Remember to dream big—because God is a big God!

experience IT YOURSELF

Write down Jeremiah 29:11 on an index card or piece of paper. Put it where you can see it every morning. Let it be a reminder to dream big for God, not letting the discouragement of others stop you from knowing and pursuing God's truth for your life.

session

5

g_5 Growth

Part 2: Loving Others

1. Describe for the rest of the group the richest insight you had from your Daily Devotions.

2. Describe the most meaningful activity you did.

3. What was it like practicing the spiritual disciplines? Did you notice whether these spiritual disciplines made any difference in how you lived your life this week?

4. What questions or concerns were raised by your Daily Devotions?

(**opening** UP)

I volunteered to go to Ecuador with my youth ministry because my friends were going. I thought it might be fun. Some of us helped with a vacation Bible school for the local kids and others helped an adult team build some houses. I got to know several elementary-school-age kids, especially two boys. We couldn't say too much directly since we didn't speak the same language, but somehow we got to know each other. They seemed to love everything we did for them. Coming home was hard, seeing how much we have compared to them. But now I can't wait to do it again. In some ways I never felt more alive.

—*Melissa, 16*

In the last session we talked about the disciplines we could put into place that would help us get to know God better. The better we know and abide in God, the more we will grow in love for him. As we love God more, we begin to live more like Jesus—which, we will see this week, means loving others.

1. When have you experienced the love of God from another person? Why do you think that person loved you that way? How did it make you feel?

2. When is the last time you served someone with the love of God? How did that make you feel? Why?

>> 1 john 4:7–12

Dear friends, let us continue to love one another, for love comes from God. Anyone who loves is born of God and knows God. But anyone who does not love does not know God—for God is love.

God showed how much he loved us by sending his only Son into the world so that we might have eternal life through him. This is real love. It is not that we loved God, but that he loved us and sent his Son as a sacrifice to take away our sins.

Dear friends, since God loved us that much, we surely ought to love each other. No one has ever seen God. But if we love each other, God lives in us, and his love has been brought to full expression through us.

read TOGETHER

Read John 4:7–12.

discuss TOGETHER

1. According to the passage, what are all the reasons we are to love others?

2. What happens to our relationship to God when we do not love others?

3. How has God modeled love for us?

community TIME

How is the love the world speaks about so much different than God's love? What are some opportunities we have each day for revealing God's love to others by our actions and words.

In prayer together, thank God for the opportunities we have for revealing him to others through acts of love. Also, ask God to help you "see" the many opportunities you have each day to be more like Jesus by serving and loving others.

experience IT TOGETHER

Now it's time for us to be examples of what it means to show love by encouraging each another. Go around the circle speaking words of encouragement to each other, being specific about our words (for example: you are always kind to others, you are always ready to help others, you are an example to me of what it means to be a fully devoted follower of Christ). After the experience is over, take time to ask each other how it felt to receive the gift of encouragement.

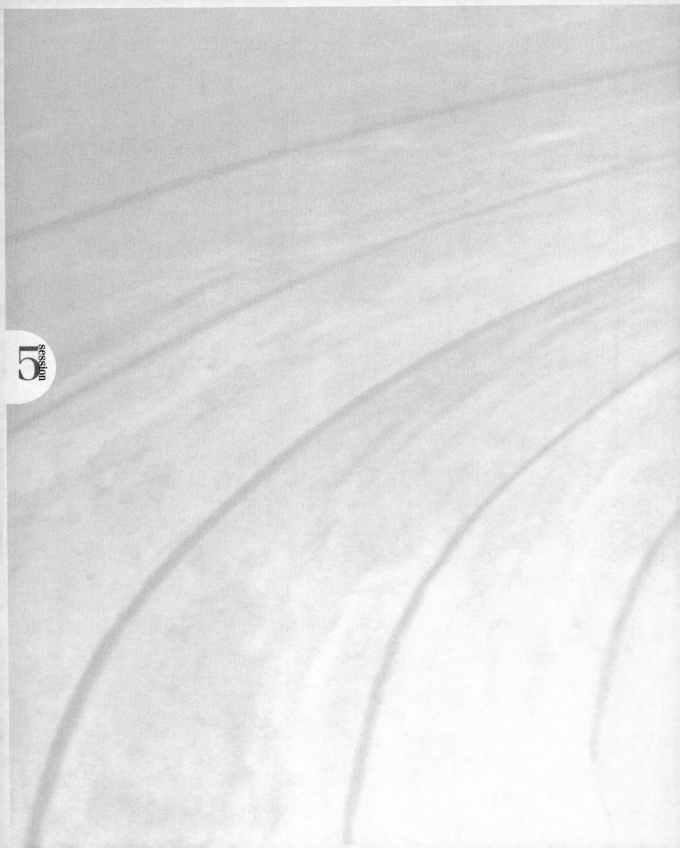

session

5

SESSION FIVE

S⁵ Growth

Part 2: Loving Others

Loving and serving others can be life-changing. In this session we will see how we can be more effective in growing in Christ-likeness by loving others.

Devotion One

d¹ Servant Leader

Who doesn't like being cheered, especially after doing something well, such as acing a test or winning a sporting event? And who doesn't like being taken care of? When people praise us and take care of us, we feel noticed, appreciated, even loved. People often praised Jesus after they were with him. One group tried to crown him king. Others put down coats and palms as he rode into Jerusalem. But Jesus kept doing unexpected things. When asked about greatness, he told his listeners to be like children—innocent, open, and trusting rather than ambitious. When given the place of honor at a dinner, he chose the lowliest seat or even went so far as to humble himself by washing Peter's feet—a real sign of a servant leader. His message is clear: If we want to grow to be like him, we must serve others. Just as we like being cheered and served, we need to learn to cheer and serve others. We need to become servant leaders—like Jesus.

see FOR YOURSELF

Highlight or underline these verses, the first from Jesus recorded in John's gospel and then from Paul's letter to the church in Philippi (a city in ancient Macedonia and now in modern Greece):

>> **john 13:15**
[Jesus speaking] "I have given you an example to follow. *Do as I have done to you.*"

>> **philippians 2:3–11**
Don't be selfish; don't live to make a good impression on others. *Be humble,* thinking of others as better than yourself. Don't think only about your own affairs, *but be interested in others,* too, and what they are doing.

Your attitude should be the same that Christ Jesus had. Though he was God, he did not demand and cling to his rights as God. He made himself nothing; he took the humble . . .

(cont.)

. . . position of a slave and appeared in human form. And in human form he obediently humbled himself even further by dying a criminal's death on a cross. Because of this, God raised him up to the heights of heaven and gave him a name that is above every other name, so that at the name of Jesus every knee will bow, in heaven and on earth and under the earth, and every tongue will confess that Jesus Christ is Lord, to the glory of God the Father.

ask YOURSELF

1. What are all the ways Jesus modeled being a servant leader?

2. Paul gives straightforward advice in his letter to the Philippians: "don't be selfish," "be humble," and "be interested in others." Would those who know you well say you are humble and you care about others? Why or why not?

3. What can you do to put into practice Paul's advice?

think FOR YOURSELF

Think about the most memorable times when someone has done something especially kind for you or when someone has served you—from simple things like a ride to school to special events like birthdays or Christmas. Then think about how you felt when you received these gifts or acts of service. Write a prayer asking God to help you be more of a servant and to provide these types of experiences to others.

experience IT YOURSELF

In the next twenty-four hours, do at least four acts of service you would not usually do. This could be as simple as letting people go first in line, stopping to pick up something that someone dropped, or volunteering to help with chores around the house. This will help us develop the habit of serving others. Ask God to give you a servant attitude and help you to see opportunities to be more like Jesus.

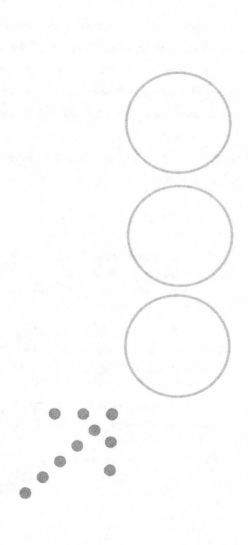

Devotion Two

d² The Power of Encouragement

Growing by learning to love and serve others can be very difficult. How do you see others as more important than yourself, especially in a world that says, "Take care of number one—you"? This seems like an impossible transformation. As we saw in the Core Values from the introductory Group Study (see page 19), spiritual transformation is God's work, not ours, and it is a process that takes time. Spiritual transformation involves our willingness to take a first step, which is often more simple than we imagine. For instance, simply being a person who encourages others can be a powerful gift to them and a step in the right direction in becoming more like Jesus.

see FOR YOURSELF

Highlight or underline in your Bible these verses from Proverbs, Hebrews (an anonymous New Testament letter), and from Paul's letter to the Philippians:

>> **proverbs 16:24**
Kind words are like honey—sweet to the soul and healthy for the body.

>> **hebrews 3:13** (TNIV)
But encourage one another daily, as long as it is called "today," so that none of you may be hardened by sin's deceitfulness.

>> **philippians 4:4–5**
Always be full of joy in the Lord. I say it again—rejoice! *Let everyone see that you are considerate in all you do.*

ask YOURSELF

1. What do you think the writer of Hebrews meant by "sin's deceitfulness"? Why do you think sin leads to being "hardened" (having a selfish heart)?

2. Why do you think it is important to make encouragement a daily habit and to let others see that we really mean what we say? What positive effect does being an encourager have in someone's life?

3. What makes our words seem believable rather than merely pretending to be nice?

4. According to Proverbs 16:24, how can kind words be like honey?

think FOR YOURSELF

In the chart below, write the names of five friends or family members on whom you can have a positive influence. Next to each name, jot down one idea of how you can be an encouragement.

>> **Name**   **Encouragement Idea**

1.

2.

3.

4.

5.

After completing the chart, write a prayer in the space below asking God to help you put these ideas into practice over the course of the next few days.

(**experience** IT YOURSELF)

This week, follow up on your encouragement ideas. In fact, email or call one or two of these people right now and give them a word of encouragement. Be specific about the qualities you see in them. For example, "I really appreciate your kind heart." Or, "You're a good friend. You're always available to listen to others." Make sure you speak the truth in love.

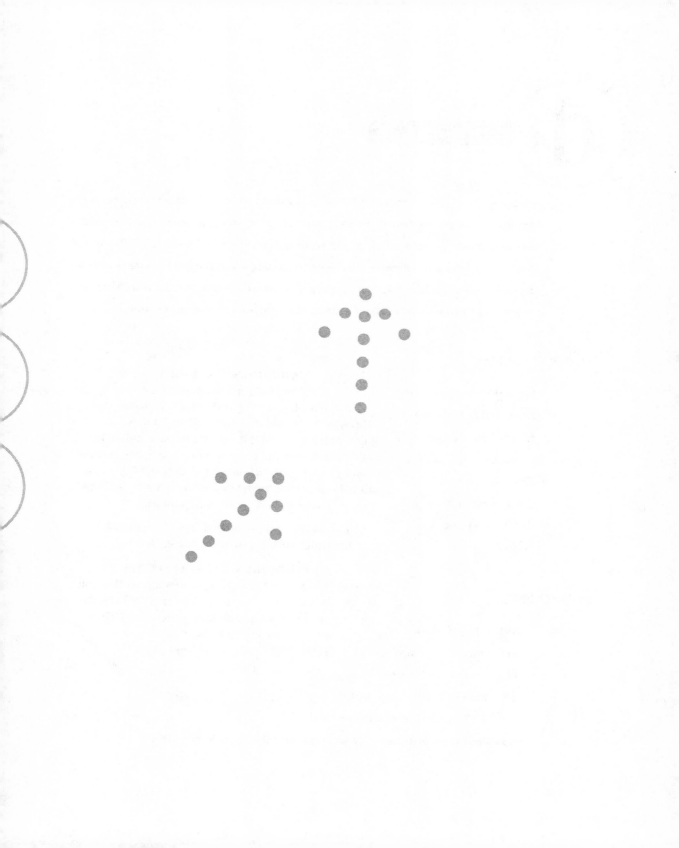

Devotion Three

d³ 2:14 Attitude

Sometimes life just seems unfair. People are mean to you; friends ignore you; parents' demands seem unreasonable. The temptation is to feel sorry for yourself and be mad—and to complain to others. Before you know it, everyone around you is in a bad mood. And here is where we discover that just as encouragement can brighten many people's days, so a bad attitude can darken the days of those we come in contact with. If we want to grow to be more like Jesus, we need to discover how to change our attitude.

see FOR YOURSELF

Highlight or underline these verses from the apostle Paul's letters to the churches in Ephesus (on the coast of modern-day Turkey) and Philippi:

ask YOURSELF

1. What do you think Paul means by his instructions to "throw off" and "put away" our old natures? What is our "new nature" and how does it get expressed? What areas does this affect in our lives?

>>
ephesians 4:21–25
Since you have heard all about him and have learned the truth that is in Jesus, throw off your old evil nature and your former way of life, which is rotten through and through, full of lust and deception. Instead, *there must be a spiritual renewal of your thoughts and attitudes.* You must display a new nature because you are a new person, created in God's likeness—righteous, holy, and true.

So put away all falsehood and "tell your neighbor the truth" because we belong to each other.

>> philippians 2:14-16 (TNIV)
Do everything without grumbling or arguing, so that you may become blameless and pure, "children of God without fault in a warped and crooked generation." Then you will shine among them like stars in the sky as you hold firmly to the word of life.

2. What do you imagine "a spiritual renewal of your thoughts and attitudes" would look like in your life?

3. Is it ever right to complain or argue? What are some ways you could express disagreement while still being "blameless and pure"?

think FOR YOURSELF

Think through the last few days of your interactions with friends and family members and write down any instances where you complained or argued about something. Reflect on how those conversations affected the people you were talking with. Also write down how you could have handled the situation expressing a "2:14 attitude." ("Do everything without complaining or arguing.") Ask God to help you have a 2:14 attitude throughout the day.

C/A 1:

C/A 2:

C/A 3:

experience IT YOURSELF

Write "2:14" on the back of your hand as a reminder for you to have a 2:14 attitude all day. Say a prayer, asking God to help you come up with alternatives to complaining and arguing.

2:14

Devotion Four

d4   The Gossip Challenge

I was sitting in the lunchroom at school when Tiffany came over and sat down. "Hey, were you at the party at Josh's this weekend? Did you hear about Anne?" she asked.

"No," I said. "What happened?" Anne was a good friend of mine, but I hadn't seen her yet at school that day.

"Well, I heard she got totally drunk and ended up being with Josh. His parents were out of town, you know," Tiffany said.

I really couldn't believe it. I knew Anne liked Josh but I couldn't imagine her just getting drunk and sleeping with him. I didn't say anything, though; I just assumed it was true. After lunch, another friend of mine, Brian, stopped me in the hallway. "Did you hear about Anne and Josh?" he asked.

"Josh and Ann! Crazy, isn't it?" I said.

"No way! I never would have expected that out of her," Brian said as he and I walked into Biology.

At the end of the day walking out to the parking lot, I saw Anne, crying by her car. "What's wrong?" I asked, trying to pretend like I hadn't heard the rumors that had been flying around all day.

"Haven't you heard what people are saying?" she asked. "Everyone says I got drunk at the party and messed around with Josh! It is totally not true—I didn't drink a thing! I was one of the last people to leave, but nothing happened between Josh and me."

I felt bad because I knew I had been a part of the gossip that was hurting her. As I apologized, I knew gossip was something I needed to try to stay away from—for my own sake and for my friends.

—*DeMara, 17*

Highlight or underline these verses from Proverbs (a collection of wise sayings in the Old Testament) and from Jesus in the gospel of Matthew:

>> **proverbs 27:6**

Wounds from a friend are better than many kisses from an enemy.

>> **proverbs 16:28**

A troublemaker plants seeds of strife; *gossip separates the best of friends.*

>> **matthew 18:15–17**

[Jesus speaking] If another believer sins against you, *go privately* and point out the fault. If the other person listens and confesses it, you have won that person back. But if you are unsuccessful, *take one or two others* with you and go back again, so that everything you say may be confirmed by two or three witnesses. If that person still refuses to listen, *take your case to the church.* If the church decides you are right, but the other person won't accept it, treat that person as a pagan or a corrupt tax collector.

a s k YOURSELF

1. How can a wound from a friend be better than kisses from an enemy? What is the result of each?

2. Have you ever experienced the "separating" power of gossip?

3. According to Jesus' process for confronting someone, what must be done first before talking to others about your concerns?

4. Even though it may be difficult, what are the advantages of going directly to a person with your concern (in other words, "wounds from a friend")?

think FOR YOURSELF

Think of a time when you heard some gossip about someone you know. How did you feel? If someone had spread the gossip about you, would you want the people who heard it to ask you about it so you could tell them the truth? How would you want people to respond to you? In the space below, ask God to help you not to listen to or be a part of gossip about someone else. When it can't be avoided, ask for courage to speak directly to the person you heard the gossip about and to find out the real truth from them.

experience IT YOURSELF

Take time to be quiet and think about whether or not you've heard or been a part of passing on gossip about someone recently. What do you need to do to set it right? For example, you might need to say you're sorry to someone or talk with them directly and find out the truth. Ask God to give you the right words to say. Make every effort to talk to that person this week.

Devotion Five

d5

Love of a Different Kind

We have explored what it means to be a servant leader and an encourager. We have also looked at the dangers of complaining, arguing, and gossiping. But what we have really been talking about is how to love others. The most radical teaching of Jesus is that we are to have the courage to show love.

see FOR YOURSELF

Highlight or underline these verses from the apostle Paul's famous passage on love:

ask YOURSELF

>> **1 corinthians 13:2–7**

If I had the gift of prophecy, and if I knew all the mysteries of the future and knew everything about everything, but didn't love others, what good would I be? And if I had the gift of faith so that I could speak to a mountain and make it move, without love I would be no good to anybody. If I gave everything I have to the poor and even sacrificed my body, I could boast about it; but *if I didn't love others, I would be of no value whatsoever.*

Love is *patient* and *kind.* Love is *not jealous* or *boastful* or *proud* or *rude.* Love does *not demand its own way.* Love is *not irritable,* and it *keeps no record* of when it has been wronged. It *is never glad about injustice* but *rejoices whenever the truth wins out.* Love *never gives up, never loses faith, is always hopeful,* and *endures through every circumstance.*

1. Paul lists some amazing accomplishments (know all mysteries, move mountains) that would be worthless without love. Think about people in the world who have accomplished success (musicians, athletes, actors). How does God view these achievements if not accomplished with an attitude of love?

2. What does the passage say about ambitions in life?

3. God's love is completely different from the world's view of love. What view of love do you need to change when it comes to loving others?

4. This is the kind of love that God has for you. How does knowing you are loved this way help you to show this kind of love to others? Why?

think FOR YOURSELF

In the space below, copy down 1 Corinthians 13:4–7 (beginning with "Love is patient . . .") but substitute your name wherever you see the word *love*. For example, if your name was Trevor, you would write, "*Trevor* is patient and kind. *Trevor* is not jealous . . ." After you are done, reflect on which of the phrases seem most unlike you. Write down your thoughts on how you want God to help you change in this area of love.

experience IT YOURSELF

Now that you've rewritten 1 Corinthians 13:4–7 with your name in it, say it out loud, asking God to help it be true in your life.

GROUP SIX

g₆
Groups

Part 1: Building Authentic Community

1. Describe for the rest of the group the richest insight you had from your Daily Devotions.

2. Describe the most meaningful activity you did.

3. How natural did it feel to do acts of service for others this week? How did people respond?

4. Were you able to encourage anyone from your list?

5. What questions or concerns were raised by your Daily Devotions?

opening UP

A few summers ago a group of guys from a high school youth ministry went on a mountain-climbing adventure. These were hard-core outdoorsmen—the harder their guides pushed them, the better they liked it. They carried their own gear, ate beans from metal cups, and washed themselves in an icy stream (when they washed themselves at all).

They set up camp at 9,000 feet and decided to take a day hike. They brought along water, nuts, and chocolates, and a few of them threw in their sleeping bags in case they decided to rest. The ten guys and their two guides took off for the valley ahead of them, destined for the 11,000-foot, snowy peak beyond. They trudged across grassy hollows and jagged overlooks. Then, out of nowhere, clouds blew in and a storm developed. They couldn't see which way they were going. The guides conferred and decided that if they attempted to return to the camp, they might get even more lost. They made the decision to stop where they were and wait until the winds died down and the sun came back up before they took another step. There was just one problem: They'd have to spend the night where they were, and only two of the ten guys had brought sleeping gear. A nighttime squall at 11,000 feet means subzero temperatures. How would they survive?

They formed a lifeline. They all faced the same direction and pressed themselves against the person in front and behind them. The two people on either end got the sleeping bags to protect their exposed side. The body heat of the group, as they postured themselves as one, saved them all from hypothermia, and maybe death.

For the last two sessions we've explored the second G, Growth, and learned the importance of spiritual training and service. Training and service can at times seem overwhelming. The good news is that God is the one doing the growing in us. And one of the ways he helps us is by giving us like-minded followers of Jesus who can offer us the encouragement, accountability, and help we need on our journey. These companions are our lifeline to keep us alive in faith, just as the ten climbers were lifelines for each other on the mountain.

1. Becoming more like Jesus happens best in the context of community (small groups). Do you believe this statement to be true? Why or why not?

2. What Christian groups have you belonged to or spent time in (such as a group of friends, a youth ministry, a serving team, a mission trip team, etc.)? How did these groups affect you? Why?

>> **philippians 2:1–4**

Is there any encouragement from belonging to Christ? Any comfort from his love? Any fellowship together in the Spirit? Are your hearts tender and sympathetic? Then make me truly happy by agreeing wholeheartedly with each other, loving one another, and working together with one heart and purpose.

Don't be selfish; don't live to make a good impression on others. Be humble, thinking of others as better than yourself. *Don't think only about your own affairs, but be interested in others,* too, and what they are doing.

>> **ephesians 4:16**

Under [Christ's] direction, the whole body is fitted together perfectly. As each part does its own special work, it helps the other parts grow, so that the whole body is healthy and growing and full of love.

read TOGETHER

Read Philippians 2:1–4 and Ephesians 4:16.

explore TOGETHER

1. How often do you see others' needs as more important than yours, and respond with tenderness and sympathy? Circle the number below that best describes your response.

1	2	3	4	5	6	7	8	9	10

I see only my needs

I see others' needs when they tell me

I see others' needs without them saying a word

2. When you help someone in need, do you get a different kind of feeling than when you meet your own needs? How is it different? Why does it feel good to help someone in need?

3. In Ephesians 4, Paul tells us that we are not *only* to look out for our own interests but also the interests of others. What is the balance that Paul is telling us to have?

4. What happens in a community when we only seek out our own interests? What happens when we only seek out the interests of others? Why is it important to have a balance of seeking out the interest of others as well as the interest of ourselves?

5. How would you rate the interest of the community in your own group (low, neutral, high)?

experience IT TOGETHER

Break up in twos and share one area in which each of you can strengthen your community. What might your group do to get to know each other better? Perhaps doing a service project together would help. Perhaps you could memorize Philippians 2:1–4 and commit to living it out while you are together. Spend time praying for each other in this area of growth.

Come back together as a large group and share a few ideas of how to build a community together. Thank God that he has called each person to be part of this community and that he has a role for everyone to play. Also pray that your group be balanced and healthy and become a good place to grow.

session

6

S 6

SESSION SIX

Groups

Part I: Building Authentic Community

Lean on me when you're not strong. I'll be your friend, I'll help you carry on. Those are the words from a hit song of the seventies, "Lean on Me." A lot of things went wrong back then, but one thing the song got right was the importance of helping one another and the value of a group of friends. But belonging to a group isn't the same thing as experiencing authentic community in Christ. In this session we are going to focus on how *authentic* (meaning "genuine" and "worthy of trust") *community* (meaning "a group with the common interest of becoming more like Jesus") provides the perfect context for experiencing growth and grace.

Devotion One

d 1   The Giver vs. the Taker

Brandon was a good athlete with many friends. In groups, he naturally captured the limelight and made people want to be around him. Eventually, many of his goals revolved around activities that brought him the attention and admiration of others. One day Brandon witnessed a kid he knew being harassed by bullies. "I don't understand why, but something just snapped. All of a sudden my goals to be popular didn't seem so all-important," says Brandon. Brandon intervened and helped his friend who was being harassed. It worked. The bullies left him alone. Although his actions made him less popular in some circles, Brandon realized, "I had to give my life some different priorities." That day God used the bullying event as an opportunity for Brandon to change from being a *taker* (someone who uses others for their own gain) to being a *giver* (someone who gave back to others).

see FOR YOURSELF

Highlight or underline these verses in your Bible:

>> **ephesians 4:1–3**
[Paul speaking] Therefore I, a prisoner for serving the Lord, beg you to *lead a life worthy of your calling,* for you have been called by God. Be humble and gentle. *Be patient with each other, making allowance for each other's faults* because of your love. Always keep yourselves united in the Holy Spirit, and bind yourselves together with peace.

>> **ephesians 6:7–8**
Work with enthusiasm, as though you were working for the Lord rather than for people. Remember that the Lord will reward each one of us for the good we do, whether we are slaves or free.

>> **acts 20:35**
[Paul speaking] "And I have been a constant example of how you can help the poor by working hard. You should remember the words of the Lord Jesus: *'It is more blessed to give than to receive.'"*

1. A *calling* is a special claim on our lives, like Jesus' claim on our lives through his death on the cross. What does it mean to "lead a life worthy of your calling"? How should our "calling" affect us?

2. A *fault* is something wrong. Why should we make "allowances" for faults in others?

3. What does Paul mean when he says it was more blessed to give than receive? How has this been true in your life?

4. When it comes to being a giver versus taker, how would you rate yourself and why? Circle the number below that best describes your response.

Taker   Giver

| 1 | 2 | 3 | 4 | 5 | 6 | 7 | 8 | 9 | 10 |

Mine is mine,   *Yours is yours,*   *Mine is*
what's yours   *and mine*   *yours*
is mine   *is mine*

t h i n k FOR YOURSELF

What can you do to make sure you have more experiences of being a *giver* and less of being a *taker?*

In the space the next page, write this verse in your own words, and replace the words "each other" with the name of someone you want to love more: *Be patient with each other, making allowance for each other's faults because of your love* (Ephesians 4:2). For example, *Be patient with Brandy, making allowances for Brandy's faults because of your love.* Then write a prayer asking God to help you to be patient, forgiving, and loving to the friend you name.

experience IT YOURSELF

In the space below, write down the names of your small group members or best friends. Say each name out loud, then listen to the Holy Spirit telling you whom you need to serve this week by writing a note, sending an email, giving a ride to school, or helping with a special project. Make a point this week to follow through on your ideas.

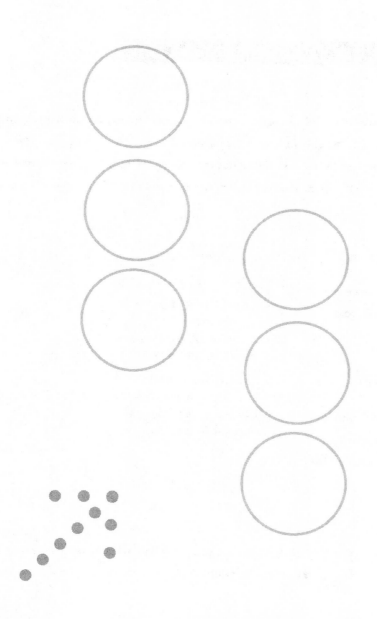

Devotion Two

A Giver's Gift: A Listening Ear

Have you ever shared a struggle with someone, only to have him or her respond: "You think *that's* bad? You should hear what happened to me!" It hurts to feel like a friend thinks more of his or her own difficulties than taking the time to listen to what you are sharing. Truly listening to and acknowledging what you heard from others is a powerful gift.

see FOR YOURSELF

Highlight or underline these verses in your Bible:

ask YOURSELF

1. What do you think Jesus meant by "Whoever has ears"?

>> **matthew 11:15**
(**TNIV**)
[Jesus speaking] *"Whoever has ears, let them hear."*

>> **james 1:19**
My dear brothers and sisters, *be quick to listen, slow to speak, and slow to get angry.*

2. When someone is speaking to you, do you really hear what he or she is saying, or are you just waiting for the chance to talk? Why?

3. What does James mean by being *quick* to listen? What would others say about how you listen?

4. How often are you fully present—focusing, listening to each word and to the heart?

5. How often do you find yourself bringing the conversation back to talking about you?

think FOR YOURSELF

Commit yourself this week to be a *listener.* That means that you look the person in the eye who is talking to you; don't let your mind go racing onto other thoughts; don't interrupt; try to enter into that person's *feelings* about what he or she is telling you; if there's a pause, don't jump in to give a quick answer or talk about yourself.

Write down your observations. Try to observe your own feelings when you listen: Did you find it hard to look the person in the eye? Did you interrupt? Did you absorb their pain? How did this conversation impact you? In the space below, write a brief letter to God, asking him to give you the ability to be fully present with others.

experience IT YOURSELF

Tomorrow, truly listen to a friend at school. Ask God to show you what your friend most needs to hear, or what God might want you to say or not to say to him or her.

Devotion Three

d³   **It Ain't Easy to Forgive**

People can hurt those around them. To be able to live in community means we have to find a way to deal with these hurts and the feelings they create in us. Jesus shows us a way of doing that. He wants us not only to *forgive* (choose not to seek revenge or justice for a wrong that has been done) but, even more, to be *reconciled* (so that the wrong done to you is forgiven and you want the best for the person). To forgive a wrong is to release the anger and overcome the desire to get back at them. It's making a relationship right again so when you see the person at home, school, or church, you don't feel angry or negative toward them. You can be friends again. That is the difference between forgiveness and reconciliation. While God *demands* that we forgive one another, he also expects us to take the next step and pursue reconciliation. Reconciliation is essential to maintaining a healthy community.

see FOR YOURSELF

Highlight or under-
line these verses in
your Bible:

>> **matthew 18:21–35**

Then Peter came to him and asked,
*"Lord, how often should I forgive someone who
sins against me? Seven times?"*

"No!" Jesus replied, *"seventy times seven!*

*"For this reason, the Kingdom of Heaven can be compared
to a king who decided to bring his accounts up to date with
servants who had borrowed money from him. In the process,
one of his debtors was brought in who owed him millions of
dollars. He couldn't pay, so the king ordered that he, his
wife, his children, and everything he had be sold to pay
the debt. But the man fell down before the king and
begged him, 'Oh, sir, be patient with me, and I will
pay it all.' Then the king was filled with pity
for him, and he released him and forgave his debt . . .*
(cont.)

. . . "But when the man left the king, he went to a fellow servant who owed him a few thousand dollars. He grabbed him by the throat and demanded instant payment. His fellow servant fell down before him and begged for a little more time. 'Be patient and I will pay it,' he pleaded. But his creditor wouldn't wait. He had the man arrested and jailed until the debt could be paid in full.

"When some of the other servants saw this, they were very upset. They went to the king and told him what had happened. Then the king called in the man he had forgiven and said, 'You evil servant! I forgave you that tremendous debt because you pleaded with me. Shouldn't you have mercy on your fellow servant, just as I had mercy on you?' Then the angry king sent the man to prison until he had paid every penny.

"That's what my heavenly Father will do to you if you refuse to forgive your brothers and sisters in your heart."

ask YOURSELF

1. What is Jesus saying about the limits of forgiveness?

2. Why was the king so angry with his servant at the end? How are we like the servant when we don't forgive someone?

3. Who do you need to forgive? Has reconciliation (where the relationship has been restored to the point where you want the best for that person) taken place? Why or why not?

4. From whom do you need to ask forgiveness?

5. Can you control how that person may respond? Does his or her response signal whether or not you should ask to be forgiven? What's more important: their response or your actions to forgive and ask for forgiveness?

think FOR YOURSELF

Ask God to give you the right words and the right heart to ask forgiveness of someone you may have hurt. If it is a situation where you are only 5 percent wrong and the other person is 95 percent wrong, you still need to ask for forgiveness of that person for your part of the percentage. In the space below, write the words God gives you to say.

experience IT YOURSELF

On your computer or a piece of paper, describe how someone has hurt you. Express not only the wrong that was done but also how it made you feel at the time and how you feel now. Think about how God has forgiven you and ask him to help you forgive this person. Now write in capital letters these words: "I FORGIVE YOU." Ask God to help you forgive the person. Then, if you are working on a computer, delete the file; if you are writing on paper, tear it up. Consider whether or not God might be inviting you to write, phone, or email that person to let them know you have forgiven them. Or ask God to give you the opportunity to see this person face-to-face so you can tell him or her in person.

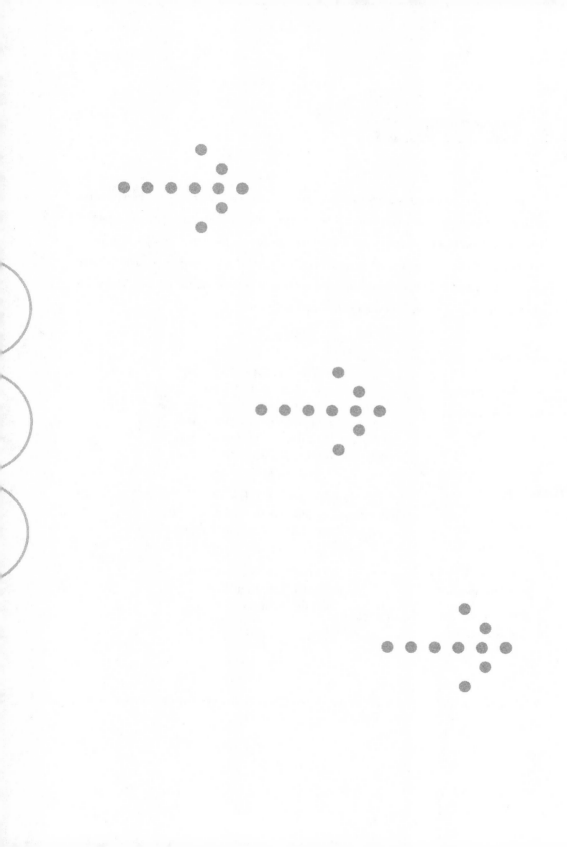

Devotion Four

d 4   Radical Love

Jesus often got into trouble for hanging out with the wrong people. He hung around with prostitutes, corrupt government officials (tax collectors), the sick, and the disabled. The more prominent citizens in the community couldn't understand why Jesus lowered his standards. Didn't he know who these people were? Jesus seemed to be saying, "If you want to truly know God, you must understand that all people matter to God. There are no important or unimportant people in God's kingdom."

see FOR YOURSELF

Highlight or under-
line these verses
in your Bible:

ask YOURSELF

1. How does
Jesus love oth-
ers? So what
does that mean for
how we are to love
and care for others?

>> **john 13:34 – 35**
[Jesus speaking] "So now I am
giving you a new commandment: Love
each other. Just as I have loved you, you
should love each other. *Your love for one
another will prove to the world that you are
my disciples.*"

>> **romans 15:6 – 7**
Then all of you can join together with one voice,
giving praise and glory to God, the Father of
our Lord Jesus Christ.

*So accept each other just as Christ
has accepted you;* then God
will be glorified.

2. Why do you think people will know we are Christ-followers if we show love to each other?

3. What does it mean to *accept* someone? What does it mean for Jesus to *accept* someone (including you)?

4. How does living in unity and accepting one another make God happy?

5. If you applied these verses to your life, how would it change the way you interact with others? With your small group?

think FOR YOURSELF

Who do you need to accept in your community to bring unity and praise to God? In the space below, write down what makes it difficult for you to accept this person. Then ask God to help you see this person the way he does and to give you the heart to accept him or her. Now write a brief prayer asking him to give you a heart like his.

experience IT YOURSELF

Think of ways you can bring unity to friends you hang out with at school, to your small group, or to the one person who is really hard for you to accept. After the two statements below, write your response.

This is what I could do or say to bring unity:

This is what I could stop doing or saying to bring unity:

Ask God to give you the opportunity and the right heart to follow through on the ideas you just wrote down.

Devotion Five

d⁵ Speaking the Truth in Love

Living in community means sometimes saying hard words to friends who need to hear them. Oftentimes, we have friends we know aren't living in ways that honor God. We need to speak the truth in love. That means having a caring heart and being willing to take the initiative, even when it is uncomfortable. It means respecting privacy and not spreading gossip or rumors that might hurt someone. It means working through the pain and fear you might have and going to that person to speak the truth in love.

see FOR YOURSELF

Highlight or underline these verses in your Bible. In the second passage, circle three words defining love that you need to work on.

>> **matthew 18:15–16**
[Jesus speaking] "*If another believer sins against you, go privately and point out the fault.* If the other person listens and confesses it, you have won that person back. But if you are unsuccessful, *take one or two others* with you and go back again, so that everything you say may be confirmed by two or three witnesses."

>> **1 corinthians 13:4–7**
Love is patient and kind. Love is not jealous or boastful or proud or rude. Love does not demand its own way. Love is not irritable, and it keeps no record of when it has been wronged. It is never glad about injustice but rejoices whenever the truth wins out. *Love never gives up, never loses faith, is always hopeful, and endures through every circumstance.*

ask YOURSELF

1. According to Matthew 18:15–16, what steps do we need to take when someone sins against us?

2. Why is it important to go in private when telling others? What response are you looking for from the person who has sinned against you?

3. According to Paul's description of love, what is the loving response when someone wrongs you?

4. What does it mean to "keep no record"?

think FOR YOURSELF

What Christian friend do you know who is involved in activities that aren't honoring to God? Have you said anything to them to let them know you care for them and what they are doing is wrong? Write their name down in big letters below, praying for God to give you the right words and the courage to speak the truth in love to them. In the space below, write down the words you need to say.

experience IT YOURSELF

Now pray again for the person you just thought about. Ask God to give you a clear leading on whether or not you should speak to that person. Be quiet and listen to God's leadings. Follow through on what God says to you. If you did not hear anything or aren't sure, ask God throughout the day what he wants you to do. Remember, speaking the truth in love is what a real friend would do.

Groups

Part 2: Receiving Love

week IN REVIEW

1. Describe for the rest of the group the richest insight you had from your Daily Devotions.

2. Describe the most meaningful activity you did.

3. How did you do last week in listening to others? Forgiving others?

4. What questions or concerns were raised by your Daily Devotions?

opening UP

When I became a Christian, my friend who had invited me to church asked me if I wanted to be a part of her small group so I decided to try it out. I was a little scared of the idea of sharing things about myself with others. I had no idea what it really meant to be in a small group, but what I found was amazing! These girls quickly became some of my best friends, and now four years later they still are! Our small group was such a safe place, I could always come and share my problems and everyone cared enough to help me through them. It felt as if we were all doing our lives together and we knew we could count on one another. I am so thankful to have experienced that community, because now I know what close relationships can really be like!

—*Alexa, 18*

1. Have you ever had someone do something good for you or give you something that made you feel unworthy? Why did it make you feel this way?

2. Has anyone stood up for you on your behalf when you were in a difficult situation? How did you respond?

read TOGETHER

Read John 8:3–11.

>> john 8:3 – 11

As [Jesus] was speaking, the teachers of religious law and Pharisees brought a woman they had caught in the act of adultery [when a married person has sex with someone other than their spouse]. They put her in front of the crowd.

"Teacher," they said to Jesus, "this woman was caught in the very act of adultery. The law of Moses says to stone her. What do you say?"

They were trying to trap him into saying something they could use against him, but Jesus stooped down and wrote in the dust . . .

(cont.)

. . . with his finger. They kept demanding an answer, so he stood up again and said, "All right, stone her. But let those who have never sinned throw the first stones!" Then he stooped down again and wrote in the dust.

When the accusers heard this, they slipped away one by one, beginning with the oldest, until only Jesus was left in the middle of the crowd with the woman. Then Jesus stood up again and said to her, "Where are your accusers? Didn't even one of them condemn you?"

"No, Lord," she said.

And Jesus said, "Neither do I. Go and sin no more."

Imagine you were part of the crowd that gathered around this confrontation, watching the religious leaders haul this woman before Jesus and then challenge him to judge the woman.

1. How did Jesus' answer put the religious leaders in a bind and force them to rethink how they understood the law and how they were treating this woman?

2. Did Jesus' answer to the woman suggest that it is all right to sin because he will always forgive?

3. How do you think the woman felt when the crowd left her? When Jesus spoke to her?

4. Imagine Jesus asking you, "Where are your accusers? Didn't even one of them condemn you?" How would you feel? Imagine Jesus saying, "Go and sin no more," directly to you. How would you respond?

5. What in the woman's response indicates she was able to receive what Jesus offered her?

experience IT TOGETHER

Discuss together why it is sometimes hard to receive love.

community TIME

Break up into pairs and pray for each other, asking God to help you become like Jesus in extending a hand of grace to others in need, but also, to become like the woman who received grace and recognized Jesus' power to forgive and set her free to go and sin no more.

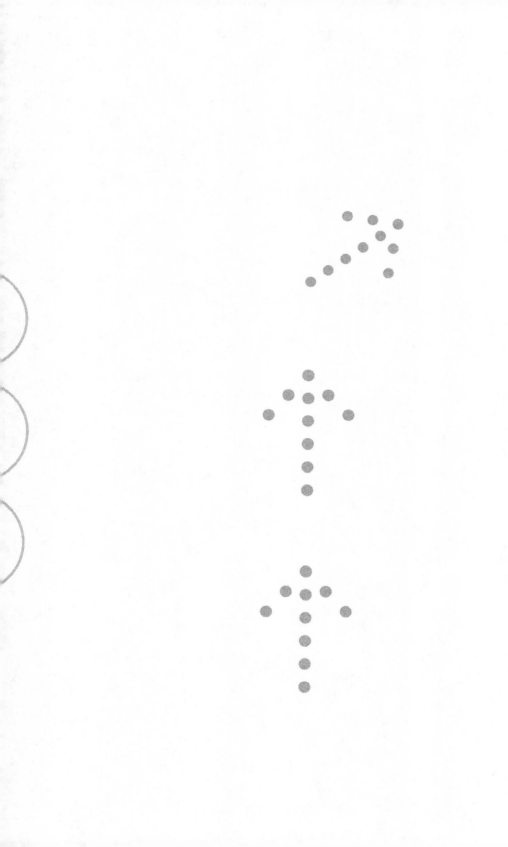

7 session

S 7

SESSION SEVEN

Groups

Part 2: Receiving Love

In the last session we examined what it means to belong to an authentic community, especially focusing on how to be a giver. But that isn't the only side of the story when it comes to real community. In fact, being a giver, for some, is the easy part. What might not come as naturally is being on the other side, that is, being the one who *receives* a blessing from someone else. In this session we focus on the importance of being humble enough to allow others to give to us, and to receive the blessing with gratitude.

Devotion One

d¹   No One Stands Alone

My parents divorced when I was young, and my mom has never been good about remembering my birthday. My sixteenth birthday was really important to me. I woke up that morning and although my dad was doing everything he could to make it a special day, I just wanted my mom to call. I waited all day, and she never did. Later that night, when I went to my small group I was pretty sad. I walked into the group and was totally surprised. They had all remembered and were throwing me a surprise party. They had gotten balloons and made a cake and really had gone all out. These girls couldn't have known how important my birthday was to me, but they made it the best birthday ever!

—*Brittany, 16*

see FOR YOURSELF

Highlight or underline these verses in your Bible:

ask YOURSELF

1. The writer of Ecclesiastes says two are better than one because when one falls, the other is there to help you up. Have you found this to be true in your life? Why or why not?

>> **ecclesiastes 4:9–12**
Two people can accomplish more than twice as much as one; they get a better return for their labor. If one person falls, the other can reach out and help. But people who are alone when they fall are in real trouble. And on a cold night, two under the same blanket can gain warmth from each other. But how can one be warm alone? A person standing alone can be attacked and defeated, but two can stand back-to-back and conquer. *Three are even better, for a triple-braided cord is not easily broken.*

>> **psalm 142:6**
Hear my cry, for I am very low. Rescue me from my persecutors, for they are too strong for me.

2. When was the last time you felt as low as the person in Psalm 142:6—in desperate need and all alone? Who did you turn to? Who was there for you? How did that have an impact on your life?

3. When you are in need of help, do you try to bear it alone, or are you able to reach up to others? Circle the number below that best describes your response.

1	2	3	4	5	6	7	8	9	10

I tell   I become   I ask for help
no one   quiet and sad   and prayer

4. Why does God's Word warn us not to try to do it all alone?

think FOR YOURSELF

Think about the people in your life who would be there for you if you were in need. Write their names below and explain what makes them so important in your life. Ask God to protect and bless them, praying for each one individually. If no one comes to mind, ask God to put someone in your life you can depend upon.

experience IT YOURSELF

Tie a braided string or twine (even better would be a braided strand of three different colors) around your ankle or wrist (Ecclesiastes 4:12) to remind you of the importance of belonging to a community. Tell a few of your close friends how thankful you are that they are part of your life and that you know they would be there for you in time of need.

Devotion Two

d 2   Let Yourself Be Known

We all have the fear that if someone really knew us, they wouldn't love us. But this is not God's design for our lives. He does not want us to hide our fears or our weaknesses. To belong to a trusting community means being willing to be honest with friends about our fears, our weaknesses, and our struggles with sin.

s e e FOR YOURSELF

Highlight or underline these verses in your Bible. Circle all the *you*'s and double underline the few words that follow them.

> **>> psalm 139:1–4**
> *O LORD, you have examined my heart and know everything about me.*
>
> You know when I sit down or stand up. You know my every thought when far away.
>
> You chart the path ahead of me and tell me where to stop and rest. Every moment you know where I am.
>
> You know what I am going to say even before I say it, LORD.
>
> **>> james 5:16**
> *Confess your sins to each other and pray for each other* so that you may be healed. The earnest prayer of a righteous person has great power and wonderful results.

a s k YOURSELF

1. How does knowing that God sees and knows everything about you make you feel? How does it affect what you are willing to reveal to others about yourself? Why?

2. Why do you think it is important to confess our sins to one another, even though God knows everything about us and forgives us?

Confession involves acknowledging the truth about your life—both positive and negative—to God, to yourself, and in appropriate ways, to others. On the three continuums below, circle the number that best describes where you stand when it comes to honest confession.

Confession to Myself

1	2	3	4	5	6	7	8	9	10

Denial—I choose
not to think
about my sins

My sins bother me

I'm fully aware
of my sins

Confession to God

1	2	3	4	5	6	7	8	9	10

God already
knows, so why
tell him?

I whisper "sorry"
now and then

I confess my
sins one by
one to God

Confession to Others

1	2	3	4	5	6	7	8	9	10

It's nobody's
business

I tell only part of the
story since I have trouble
trusting others

I tell the
whole truth

Based on your responses, consider what it would take for you to move each response farther up the scale. Mark an X on each continuum indicating where you would like to be. Ask God to help you be open to receive love.

Email or call a trusted friend and ask for prayer about a burden, sin, or weakness you are facing. Tell them how thankful you are they are there to help you. Remember, God wants you to have community with others.

Devotion Three

d³ Hide-and-Seek

One of my favorite memories as a kid was playing hide-and-seek in the dark. A whole gang of us would go running off in different directions and hide under logs or behind cars. But the most fun part was the suspense of waiting in the dark, knowing "It" was lurking somewhere out there trying to find me. Then, when I'd been found, I'd feel equal amounts of regret and relief, because being alone in the dark was really scary and it was comforting to know that someone found me.

—Jay, 17

see FOR YOURSELF

Highlight or underline these verses in your Bible. Circle all the unlikely places where God is "there."

ask YOURSELF

1. How does it make you feel to know that you cannot hide from God? Does it make you feel safer, or does it cause you to be fearful? Why?

>> **psalm 139:7–12**

I can never escape from your spirit! *I can never get away from your presence!*

If I go up to heaven, you are there; if I go down to the place of the dead, you are there.

If I ride the wings of the morning, if I dwell by the farthest oceans,

even there your hand will guide me, and your strength will support me.

I could ask the darkness to hide me and the light around me to become night—

but even in darkness I cannot hide from you.

To you the night shines as bright as day. Darkness and light are both alike to you.

2. Why do you think we like to hide from others in our lives?

3. What are the benefits of "being found" when the truth about us comes out?

4. What is one thing people assume about you that you wish they wouldn't?

(**think** FOR YOURSELF)

Look at what you circled above in Psalm 139. Think about what it means for God to know all that you do and for him to be with you wherever you go. Think about what in your life would be the equivalent of all the places you go where God is still present. For example, when you are sad or alone, when you are in a frightening experience, when you are laughing and hanging out with friends, when you are with your boyfriend or girlfriend (if you have one). Then ask God to help you not to hide yourself from those close to you—good Christian friends, your youth minister, family members. In the space below, write down the names of people you want to reveal more of yourself to and pray for opportunities this week to open up your life more to them.

(**experience** IT YOURSELF)

Close your hands and make two fists. Let one hand represent God and the other represent the friends in your life. With your eyes closed, pray and visualize yourself completely alone with no one else in your life. Then slowly open one hand, representing that you are never alone, that God is there for you. Thank God that you are never alone. Then slowly open up your other hand, saying you are opening yourself up to others, thanking God that he's put others in your life. Say the names out loud of some Christian friends or youth leaders who care about you.

Devotion Four

d4 Community Breakers

Real care from others sometimes can be painful. Just as some awful-tasting medicine actually makes us better, being confronted with a truth we either don't want to see or hear for ourselves can help us grow spiritually. If we are not willing to receive correction from people God has put in our lives, real community breaks down.

see FOR YOURSELF

Highlight or underline these verses in your Bible:

ask YOURSELF

1. What is meant by "iron sharpens iron"? What does it mean for a friend to sharpen you?

>> **proverbs 27:17**
As iron sharpens iron, a friend sharpens a friend.

>> **proverbs 27:5**
An open rebuke [a sharp criticism done in person] is better than hidden love!

>> **ephesians 4:15** (TNIV)
Instead, *speaking the truth in love,* we will in all things grow up into him who is the Head, that is, Christ.

>> **hebrews 12:11**
No discipline is enjoyable while it is happening— it is painful! But afterward there will be a quiet harvest of right living for those who are trained in this way.

2. How does rebuke from a friend show you that they really care about you?

3. If you have received appropriate correction from friends, how did it make you feel?

4. Have you received inappropriate correction from your friends? How did that make you feel?

5. According to Hebrews, what is supposed to result from being corrected by others?

think FOR YOURSELF

Think about the last time someone challenged you with truth about you that was hard to hear. Did you see it as a gesture of love and that they were caring for you? Was your heart open? Or did it make you angry? Take a moment to ask God to give you an open heart to correction. Below, write down the names of people you trust enough to receive from them a challenge or correction. Again, thank God for the people he's placed in your life to help you be like him.

experience IT YOURSELF

Email Proverbs 27:17 to a few good friends who help sharpen you. Send them a note to thank them for being the kind of friends they are and encourage them to keep on sharpening you. If you haven't experienced this yet, you may want to invite some of your good friends to speak truth into your life so you can be sharpened.

Devotion Five

d5

Having the Right Expectations

Your small group of Christians is a great place for life change and spiritual transformation. But your group cannot meet all your needs and may sometimes disappoint you. Just as you are a person with weaknesses and problems, so is each person in the group. It is too much to expect that every person in the group will be your close friend. But that doesn't mean you can't still experience authentic community and show Christ's love to one another. It is challenging to belong to an intimate group. But the rewards are deep— a deeper love for others and for Christ.

see FOR YOURSELF

Highlight or underline these verses in your Bible:

>> **romans 3:23**
For all have sinned; all fall short of God's glorious standard.

>> **psalm 107:1**
Give thanks to the LORD, for he is good! *His faithful love endures forever.*

ask YOURSELF

1. What does the passage in Romans remind us about all people (including yourself)?

2. How does this keep our expectations of others in balance?

3. What does it mean to say God's love "endures forever"? In what ways have you seen that God's love is trustworthy?

think FOR YOURSELF

God tells us he will never let us down or leave us alone, and that his love is everlasting. In the space below, write how knowing this truth enables you to love others. Then write how knowing it helps you to receive love. Thank God for his everlasting love, and for his plan for you to live in community.

experience IT YOURSELF

Write the word *friend* on an index card or on your computer. Take a moment to pray and thank God for the friends in your life, naming them. Then look at the word *friend* again and write on the card, "God is my best friend," to remind you that he is always there for you. Let these two reminders free you to be in community with others, and at the same time, help you to realize that God will always be there for you.

REMEMBER:
Bring a shoe box
to the next
Group Study!

8 session

g₈ Gifts

Part 1: Discovering Your Gifts

1. Describe for the rest of the group the richest insight you had from your Daily Devotions.

2. Describe the most meaningful activity you did.

3. How did you do last week in your attempts to reveal more of yourself to others?

4. What questions or concerns were raised by your Daily Devotions?

opening UP

Jen participated in her first mission project to the Dominican Republic when she was in tenth grade. Those two weeks of service to other people began to shape in her a passion for mission and a stronger desire to serve others. Over the next few years Jen participated regularly as a leader in her church youth ministry and took risks to share her faith with and serve her friends at school. Her youth pastor helped her to understand that by experimenting in different kinds of ministries, by serving her friends, sharing her faith, and caring for people, she would have more and more opportunities to discover how God had uniquely gifted her.

Jen is now in her first year of college. She is studying to be a nurse and wants to use her nursing degree to serve needy people in Africa. Jen knows her gifts are in leadership, serving of others, and evangelism. She discovered her gifts over the course of a few years as she grew in her faith, practiced the things she was learning at her church, took a spiritual gifts assessment, and asked her friends and family what they saw in her.

Spiritual gifts are *divine enablements*—special God-given abilities—that God gives to each of his followers in order to help them do his work on earth. In other words, God made you with a special gift so you can do your part in his ministry. How awesome is that—to not only be a part of God's plan to change the world, but to be gifted at what we do!

For the last two sessions we have explored the importance of living in authentic community with others in a small group. As we give and receive care in community, we begin to discover that God has given us special abilities called *spiritual gifts* that contribute to the equipping and building of God's community. In this session we're going to explore how each of us can find out what our spiritual gift(s) might be and how to use them to do our part to serve in the local church.

1. Think of people who are active in your church. What special abilities have you seen demonstrated as they perform their ministries?

2. What special abilities, or areas someone is especially good in, have you noticed among those in this group?

read TOGETHER

Read 1 Corinthians 12:1, 4–7, and 1 Peter 2:9.

>> **1 corinthians 12:1, 4–7**

And now, dear brothers and sisters, I will write about the special abilities the Holy Spirit gives to each of us. . . .

Now there are *different* kinds of spiritual gifts, but it is the *same* Holy Spirit who is the source of them all. There are *different* kinds of service in the church, but it is the *same* Lord we are serving. There are *different* ways God works in our lives, but it is the *same* God who does the work through all of us. A spiritual gift is given to each of us as a means of helping the entire church.

>> **1 peter 2:9**

You are a chosen people. You are a kingdom of priests, God's holy nation, his very own possession. This is so you can show others the goodness of God, for he called you out of the darkness into his wonderful light.

explore TOGETHER

1. From 1 Corinthians, name all the things mentioned as "different" and all the things mentioned as the "same." What does this reveal about how God works with us?

2. Paul says each of us has been given a spiritual gift. What is the purpose of spiritual gifts?

3. What do you know about spiritual gifts? What are some of the spiritual gifts you are aware of?

4. Imagine being given a gift by someone who really loves you and never opening it up! How would it make the giver of the gift feel? How do you think God feels about us not opening up the gifts he's given us?

5. A priest is a mediator between God and people, representing the people to God and declaring God's acts to the people. Have you ever considered yourself a priest or minister? How do Paul's words help you to see your purpose in the church?

experience IT TOGETHER

Pull out the shoe box you brought with you. Using a large sheet of white paper and some tape, wrap only the lid in the paper (so you can write on it later). You will be using this box in the next two weeks to help you learn more about your spiritual gifts.

community TIME

The box represents you and your life as the container for the spiritual gifts God has given you to minister to the church, the body of Christ. Pray together, asking God to show you how to be a minister, how to recognize your spiritual gifts, and how to serve others by using your gifts. Write your name on the outside of your gift box. Ask God to help you discover and understand the gifts you are to use in the body of Christ.

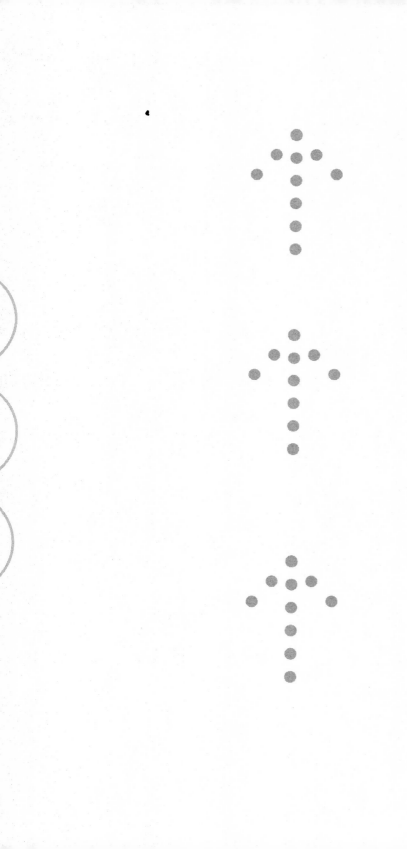

8 session

SESSION EIGHT

S 8

Gifts

Part 1: Discovering Your Gifts

In the last session we talked about the importance of authentic community and how it demands a lot of "giving" love as well as "receiving" love. Sometimes that kind of love can hurt, and sometimes that kind of love is hard to receive. This way of living brings growth and helps us become more like Jesus. In this session we're going to explore how each of us can find and understand that special way God has called us to contribute our part to kingdom work, and to building the church. God has gifted each believer with at least one spiritual gift. In these devotions we will begin to discover what this means for us.

Devotion One

d¹ Use Me

When I learned about spiritual gifts, I found out I had the gift of encouragement. At first I was a little disappointed because I wasn't sure what I could really do with that gift. But lately I have been learning that there are a lot of ways to use my gift. I started to notice what people were feeling—when they seemed sad, scared, or frustrated. It was amazing to see how just a few kind words or an encouraging note could help them.

One time, a friend of mine from church who is a great leader was going to be teaching a Bible study at our school during lunch. As I talked to her the morning before she was supposed to lead the group, she seemed really nervous. She even said she wasn't sure if she was the right person to be doing this. It was so easy for me to encourage her though, to tell her I knew she was the right person and that she was going to do a great job. And during the Bible study, she did do a great job! She made a huge difference by using her leadership that day. She told me later that she wouldn't have been able to do it if I hadn't been there for her and encouraged her. I knew then that my gifts made a difference— that my gifts could work together with other people's gifts to honor God.

—Trevor, 16

see FOR YOURSELF

Highlight or under-line these verses in your Bible from the apostle Paul:

>> **1 corinthians 1:7**
Now *you have every spiritual gift you need* as you eagerly wait for the return of our Lord Jesus Christ.

>> **2 timothy 1:6**
This is why I remind you to *fan into flames the spiritual gift God gave you.*

>> **1 timothy 4:14**
Do not neglect the spiritual gift you received.

1. What does this say about you having your own unique spiritual gift?

2. Twice Paul encourages Timothy in using his spiritual gift. What do Paul's comments imply regarding our responsibility for our spiritual gifts?

Pastor Bill Hybels has written a simple and powerful prayer he calls the "Use Me" prayer: *Use me, God. Show me what my part is in the transformation of the world. Take hold of my head, my heart, and my hands and use me for your purposes.* Rewrite this prayer below, expanding on the various ways God is, and can be, using you. (For example, "Lord, use me to reach Brittany, since she seems to be asking lots of spiritual questions right now.")

Write "use me" on an index card or somewhere you'll be able to see it throughout the day (like on one of your book covers). Make it your theme throughout the day. Begin the day with a "use me" prayer. Make yourself available to be used at home or at school or wherever you are. Throughout the day say "use me" prayers before you start conversations or begin activities. Make your life an exercise in being used by God.

Devotion Two

d²   Putting the Pieces Together

Discovering your spiritual gifts is an exciting journey. The first step is to explore the different experiences, talents, and passions we have, as well as what affirmation we have received from others who know us well. Discovering your gifts takes time and self-examination. Be patient, knowing that God will reveal to you what your spiritual gifts are. Also, we don't have to wait until we know our exact gifts before we can serve. We all share a calling to certain areas of ministry: evangelism, mercy, giving. But as we serve in these general areas, God will reveal our special gift he has given us.

see FOR YOURSELF

Highlight or underline these verses in your Bible. Then circle each gift.

>> **romans 12:4–8**
*Just as our bodies have many parts
and each part has a special function, so
it is with Christ's body. We are all parts of his
one body, and each of us has different work to do.
And since we are all one body in Christ, we belong
to each other, and each of us needs all the others.*

God has given each of us the ability to do certain things well.
So if God has given you the ability to prophesy, speak out
when you have faith that God is speaking through you.
If your gift is that of serving others, serve them well.
If you are a teacher, do a good job of teaching. If your gift
is to encourage others, do it! If you have money, share
it generously. If God has given you leadership ability,
take the responsibility seriously. And if you have
a gift for showing kindness to others,
do it gladly.

>> **ephesians 4:11–12**
He is the one who gave these
gifts to the church: the apostles,
the prophets, the evangelists, and
the pastors and teachers. *Their
responsibility is to equip God's
people to do his work and
build up the church,*
the body of Christ.

1. What are the gifts mentioned by Paul in Ephesians 4 on page 174? What is the shared purpose of these gifts?

2. What gifts does Paul use as examples in Romans 12 on page 174? In those examples, what is Paul saying about how we are to exercise our gifts?

think FOR YOURSELF

A good way to understand what your gifts may be is to look at how God wired you up in a special way to be a difference-maker for him. How he made you is not a mistake. A good way to get a clear idea of what gifts you possess is to ask yourself these four questions—like four corner pieces of the puzzle.

CORNER PIECE 1 *(your passion)*: What do you have passion for? A good way to understand this is to ask your-self, "What activities do I do where I feel like I'm making a difference or feel that God is really pleased with what I'm doing?" Another way to think about it is to consider what it is you like to think a lot about—maybe it even keeps you up at night.

CORNER PIECE 2 *(your talents)*: What are you good at? Sports? Music? Writing? Acting? Computers? Think over your life and consider things you do that you are good at.

CORNER PIECE 3 *(your experiences)*: What experiences have you had when you really felt excited while doing some activity? What experience have you had where you made a difference and had success? For example, a mission trip you went on, or certain work project at school or work. What made the experience meaningful? Was it the people you were serving—kids, the poor, the elderly? Was it the location you were serving at—the inner city, another country?

CORNER PIECE 4 *(what others say)*: This corner piece is to help you think about how others affirmed you for doing a good job in the activities you've been a part of. Look for a pattern in what others say about your gifts and skills.

Once you understand these four corner pieces, they provide an inside look at how God wired you. All of these four pieces are not a mistake; they all point to what your spiritual gifts may be. In the spaces below, as best you can, write your responses to all four statements. This will help you get a picture of what your gifts may be.

Corner Piece 1: I have a passion for . . .

Corner Piece 2: My talents include . . .

Corner Piece 3: I felt like I was really making a difference when . . .

Corner Piece 4: I have been affirmed by others when I . . .

experience IT YOURSELF

On the outside of your gift box, write a few sentences in each corner describing what you've learned about your corner pieces. Transfer what you wrote above onto the corners of your box. (You'll write in the middle of the box later so leave that area blank.) Ask God to give you an opportunity to discover and use your spiritual gifts. Ask him to help you put the four corner pieces together to see the unique picture of how God wired you to be a difference-maker for him.

Devotion Three

d³ — Finding the Right Gift

You are closing in on knowing more clearly what special abilities God has given you. Of course, there is no definitive listing of spiritual gifts. God is creative. Any ability consistently used by the Holy Spirit to build up the body of Christ (the church) could be called a spiritual gift. But the Bible does mention quite a few, and here we will explore the spiritual gifts mentioned or shown in Scripture in order to see what your role in building the body of Christ might be.

see FOR YOURSELF

Highlight or underline these verses in your Bible:

ask YOURSELF

1. Look over the spiritual gifts mentioned. How do they work together to serve the church?

>> **1 corinthians 12:8 – 11**
To one person the Spirit gives the *ability to give wise advice;* to another he gives the *gift of special knowledge.* The Spirit gives *special faith* to another, and to someone else he gives the *power to heal* the sick. He gives one person the *power to perform miracles,* and to another the *ability to prophesy.* He gives someone else the *ability to know whether it is really the Spirit of God* or another spirit that is speaking. Still another person is given the *ability to speak in unknown languages,* and another is given the *ability to interpret what is being said.* It is the one and only Holy Spirit who distributes these gifts. He alone decides which gift each person should have.

2. Why is it important to Paul to emphasize that the Holy Spirit is the one who decides who gets what gift?

Below is a list of spiritual gifts mentioned or described in the Bible. Put one of the three numbers listed below before each gift to indicate how it describes you.

0 — I have never demonstrated this gift.

1 — I have performed (or could perform) this function adequately, but I'm not sure it's one of my gifts.

2 — I have this gift and/or think I could perform very well if I had the opportunity.

____ **Administration:** ability to organize people and tasks

____ **Apostleship:** ability to start and oversee new ministries or churches

____ **Craftsmanship:** ability to design and construct items for ministry

____ **Creative Communication:** ability to express God's truth through the arts

____ **Discernment:** ability to distinguish the truth from falsehood, true motives, or the presence of evil

____ **Encouragement:** ability to strengthen and comfort

____ **Evangelism:** ability to communicate the gospel in a compelling way

____ **Faith:** ability to act on God's promises with unwavering belief

____ **Giving:** ability to give resources with cheerfulness and generosity

____ **Healing:** ability to bring people toward wholeness

____ **Helps:** ability to joyfully serve others

____ **Hospitality:** ability to welcome and nurture others

____ **Intercession:** ability to pray intensely and often for others

____ **Interpretation:** ability to make known a message spoken in an unknown language

___ **Knowledge:** ability to understand truth through biblical insight

___ **Leadership:** ability to cast vision, motivate, and direct people to accomplish tasks

___ **Mercy:** ability to help and comfort those who are suffering

___ **Miracles:** ability to perform supernatural actions that glorify Christ

___ **Prophecy:** ability to speak God's message to a particular issue or event

___ **Shepherding:** ability to nurture and guide people toward maturity

___ **Teaching:** ability to explain clearly God's truth

___ **Tongues:** ability to speak or pray in an unknown language

___ **Wisdom:** ability to apply spiritual insight to specific issues or situations

experience IT YOURSELF

Look at the four corners of your spiritual gift box. Using the spiritual gift list above, focus on those you rated with the number two. Of these, choose two or three that are consistent with what you wrote on the corners of your box or that you feel very sure could be your spiritual gifts. Write these two to three gifts in the center of your gift box. Then ask God to reveal to you if these are your gifts, as you discover more about yourself over the next weeks. Ask others in your small group if they see these gifts in your life. Talk to your small group leader about ways to use these gifts to help you know for sure if they are your spiritual gifts.

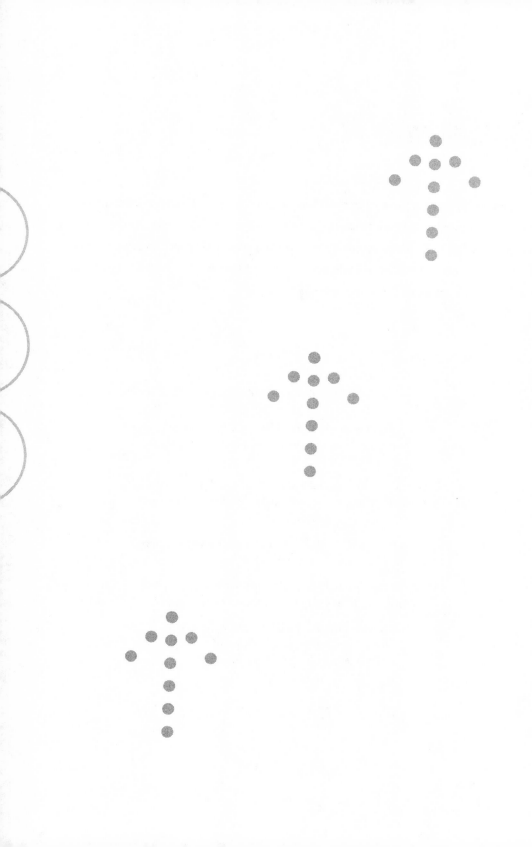

Devotion Four

d 4 **Who Am I?**

Often when we start to realize that God has given us special abilities, we may think, *Who am I that God would want to use me?* This is the same question Moses asked when God wanted to use his life to rescue his people from slavery in Egypt and bring them to the Promised Land. We need to understand that God knows who we are, he made us this way, and he wants to use us in a powerful way.

s e e FOR YOURSELF

Highlight or underline these verses from the second book in the Bible:

>> **exodus 3:10 – 15; 4:1**

[God said to Moses] "Now go, for I am sending you to Pharaoh. You will lead my people, the Israelites, out of Egypt."

"But who am I to appear before Pharaoh?" Moses asked God. "How can you expect me to lead the Israelites out of Egypt?"

Then God told him, "I will be with you. And this will serve as proof that I have sent you:

When you have brought the Israelites out of Egypt, you will return here to worship God at this very mountain."

But Moses protested, "If I go to the people of Israel and tell them, 'The God of your ancestors has sent me to you,' they won't . . .

(cont.)

. . . believe me. They will ask, 'Which god are you talking about? What is his name?' Then what should I tell them?"

God replied, "I Am the One Who Always Is. Just tell them, 'I Am has sent me to you.'" God also said, "Tell them, 'The Lord, the God of your ancestors—the God of Abraham, the God of Isaac, and the God of Jacob—has sent me to you.'" . . .

But Moses protested again, "Look, they won't believe me! They won't do what I tell them. They'll just say, 'The Lord never appeared to you.'"

ask YOURSELF

1. Have you ever felt like Moses did: overwhelmed and not sure why God would want to use you for his kingdom work? What makes you feel that way?

2. What makes you feel inadequate about serving God?

3. What fears do you have about what others may say about you when you are serving God?

think FOR YOURSELF

Moses first wondered, "Who am I?" then "How can I lead?" and finally "Why should they believe me?" In the space below, write out the questions you most identify with. Ask God to give you courage and confidence to be used by him, to do his plan for your life, knowing he'll be with you the way he was with Moses.

experience IT YOURSELF

Write 2 Corinthians 12:9 on an index card: "My gracious favor is all you need. My power works best in your weakness." Place it in your gift box. Say a prayer, letting God know that even though you may feel weak and afraid at times, your life is available to be used by him.

Devotion Five

d5

Celebrating Others' Gifts

Jamie and Natalie used to sit at the piano and compose fun songs together. As they grew up and moved into high school, Jamie grew in talent and learned she had the spiritual gift of creative communication. She began playing in special church programs and even on a local Christian radio station. Instead of supporting her friend's success, Natalie felt hurt and jealous that her best friend had abandoned her to follow her dreams. It didn't take long for their friendship to end because Natalie could not find a way to celebrate her friend's success. Our spiritual gifts are designed to be used for doing God's work, but human jealousy and hurts can still show up and keep us from doing our part—and sometimes even others' parts—in kingdom work. Instead, we need to learn how to celebrate each other's gifts, and recognize our own contribution and unique gifts as well.

see FOR YOURSELF

Highlight or underline these verses in your Bible:

>> james 3:13–18

If you are wise and understand God's ways, live a life of steady goodness so that only good deeds will pour forth. And if you don't brag about the good you do, then you will be truly wise! But if you are bitterly jealous and there is selfish ambition in your hearts, don't brag about being wise. That is the worst kind of lie. For jealousy and selfishness are not God's kind of wisdom. Such things are earthly, unspiritual, and motivated by the Devil. *For wherever there is jealousy and selfish ambition, there you will find disorder and every kind of evil.*

But the wisdom that comes from heaven is first of all pure. It is also peace loving, gentle at all times, and willing to yield to others. It is full of mercy and good deeds. It shows no partiality and is always sincere. And those who are peacemakers will plant seeds of peace and reap a harvest of goodness.

1. According to James 3, where do envy and selfish ambition come from? What are the results of their work?

2. What is the alternative to jealousy and selfishness? What does this say about celebrating the different spiritual gifts God has given to others?

3. Why are peacemakers so highly valued?

think FOR YOURSELF

Reflect on the following questions: How often do you wish you were like someone else? Do you find yourself being jealous over others? What would it take for you to be completely at peace with how God has gifted you, and how God has gifted others? In the space below, list the gifts you see God is honoring in those in your small group. Ask God to give you a heart to celebrate these gifts with them. Then write down the gifts you think God has given you. Ask God to give you peace about how he has made you and your unique giftedness. Thank him for your own gift(s).

experience IT YOURSELF

In your gift box, place a card with the name of someone in your group whose gift you could celebrate. Thank God that he has made everyone in the body of Christ different, and yet unites us for his glory. Now write an encouraging note or email to that person. Look for ways where you can start to encourage others in the gifts God has given them.

GROUP NINE

g₉

Gifts

Part 2: Using Your Gifts

1. Describe for the rest of the group the richest insight you had from your Daily Devotions.

2. Describe the most meaningful activity you did.

3. What do you think are your spiritual gifts? How might your gifts be used in the church to help others?

4. What questions or concerns were raised by your Daily Devotions?

opening UP

Last week in my small group, my leader taught us about spiritual gifts. He read 1 Corinthians 12 and explained to us that God has given us all gifts. These gifts allow me to be a part of the church—to serve and make a difference in the best way that I can. I learned that day that we are all members of the body of Christ, and we all make up different parts of it. It was so exciting to hear how everyone is important—that we all have a role to play in God's plan to reach the world. I can't wait to find out what gifts God has given me; then I can learn where they fit into my youth ministry and how I can use them.

—*Tory, 13*

What would happen if every Christian really used his or her gifts for the good of others? Wouldn't it be amazing to be a part of a church like that? It happened in the first-century church, recounted by Luke in Acts 2. It can happen again. God can use your generation to be an example to all believers. It begins with you using your gifts to love God and love others.

1. Share an experience when you were part of a group that accomplished something together that no one member of the group could have accomplished alone.

2. What spiritual gifts do you think are needed for a group or church to fully function the way God intended it to? What hinders a group from reaching its full potential?

Read Acts 2:21–47 and Romans 12:4–5.

>> acts 2:41 – 47

Those who believed what Peter said were baptized and added to the church—about three thousand in all. They joined with the other believers and devoted themselves to the apostles' teaching and fellowship, sharing in the Lord's Supper and in prayer.

A deep sense of awe came over them all, and the apostles performed many miraculous signs and wonders. And all the believers met together constantly and shared everything they had. They sold their possessions and shared the proceeds with those in need. They worshiped together at the Temple each day, met in homes for the Lord's Supper, and shared their meals with great joy and generosity—all the while praising God and enjoying the goodwill of all the people. And each day the Lord added to their group those who were being saved.

>> romans 12:4 – 5

Just as our bodies have many parts and each part has a special function, so it is with Christ's body. We are all parts of his one body, and each of us has different work to do. And since we are all one body in Christ, we belong to each other, and each of us needs all the others.

explore TOGETHER

1. What did the church members "devote themselves to"? Why are these important?

2. What do you think outsiders thought of the church of that day? What made it such an effective community?

3. How hard would it have been to be a Christ-follower in that church and not have gotten involved? Why? Why does the church today have so many spectators and so few participants? What do you think the reason is for that?

4. In what ways did the Acts 2 church function as "one body"? What kind of commitment and attitude do you think was needed for the Acts 2 church to run well?

5. According to Romans 12, how does comparing spiritual gifts to the different parts of a human body help us understand how we are to use our spiritual gifts?

6. In what ways is your group or student ministry similar to and different from the church described in Acts 2?

experience IT TOGETHER

Wouldn't it be amazing to have been a part of the church in Acts 2? When we read this, we think of it as something that could only have happened a long time ago. But it can still happen today! God has not changed. Every believer has the power to serve and use his or her gifts for the common good in amazing ways. Imagine if all Christ-followers decided to take responsibility for their own giftedness. Imagine what would happen in your life, in your friends' lives, in your youth ministry, in the church. Take some time to discuss and envision what this might look like for your youth ministry.

community TIME

Break up into groups of two or three, and share with one another what gifts you believe God has given each person. After you finish, come back together and reflect on how these gifts can be used in your student ministry. Pray about how God might use each of you to bring about the Acts 2 church to your group, and to your generation. Ask God to help you see how to use your gifts more effectively this week in making the Acts 2 church a reality. Pray together and thank God for the gifts he's given each of you, and ask him to show you how he wants you to use your unique gifts.

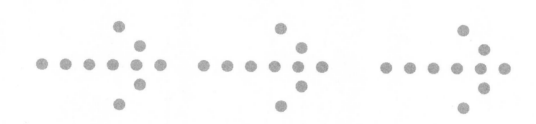

session

9

SESSION NINE

S 9

Gifts

Part 2: Using Your Gifts

In the last session we examined how each of us can discover that extraordinary way God has called us to contribute our part to the body of Christ. In this session we'll focus on how to use the spiritual gifts God has given us.

Devotion One

d1   The Right Purpose

God has given each believer the right gift for the right purpose. You are no exception. Every believer is given at least one spiritual gift for the advancement of God's purposes. Our part is to be willing to be used by God for his purposes. This includes discovering your gifts and praying about how to use them to help others bring honor to God.

see FOR YOURSELF

Highlight or underline these verses in your Bible:

>> **1 peter 4:10–11**
God has given gifts to each of you from his great variety of spiritual gifts. Manage them well so that God's generosity can flow through you. Are you called to be a speaker? Then speak as though God himself were speaking through you. Are you called to help others? Do it with all the strength and energy that God supplies. Then God will be given glory in everything through Jesus Christ.

>> **ephesians 4:12–13**
Their responsibility [every believer] *is to equip God's people to do his work and build up the church,* the body of Christ, until we come to such unity in our faith and knowledge of God's Son that we will be mature and full grown in the Lord, measuring up to the full stature of Christ.

>> **1 corinthians 12:7**
A spiritual gift is given to each of us as a means of helping the entire church.

1. In 1 Peter 4, Peter is very clear on how we are to use our gifts. What is he clear about?

2. What does Paul in Ephesians describe as the ultimate outcome of using our gifts?

3. How does using our spiritual gifts build unity in the body?

In the space below, write how you think God wants you to serve in the work of your student ministry? If you are not a part of the church, ask God to show you the right church or ministry for you to serve in. Ask God to continually show you what your spiritual gifts are, and what your responsibilities are to help equip other believers (one of the functions of spiritual gifts) by providing you with serving opportunities.

On an index card or a piece of paper, write down where you currently serve (or where you would like to serve) in the church, using your gifts. For example, youth ministry, missions, or children's ministry. If you are not currently serving or aren't sure where you'd like to serve, put a question mark on the card. Place this note in your gift box, and ask God to continually show you what your gifts may be and where you might use them to serve others. Talk to a youth leader or small group leader within the next two weeks and ask for help to discover your gifts and find ways to use them in the church.

d² The Right Gift

Sometimes we are tempted to believe some gifts are more important than others. We might even feel like our gift isn't that important, or desire someone else's gift. But this is not the plan God has for us. He made you the way you are and intends to use you the way he made you. Take encouragement that God did not make a mistake with the gift he has given you!

see FOR YOURSELF

Highlight or underline these verses in your Bible:

ask YOURSELF

1. Paul uses the imagery of the human body to describe the functioning of Christ's body, the church. Why is this a fitting image for how the church should function? What does it mean to be one body?

>> **1 corinthians 12:18–27**

God made our bodies with many parts, and he has put each part just where he wants it. What a strange thing a body would be if it had only one part! Yes, there are many parts, but only one body. The eye can never say to the hand, "I don't need you." The head can't say to the feet, "I don't need you."

In fact, some of the parts that seem weakest and least important are really the most necessary. . . . If one part suffers, all the parts suffer with it, and if one part is honored, all the parts are glad.

Now all of you together are Christ's body, and each one of you is a separate and necessary part of it.

2. Why is it important for people to have different gifts?

3. In 1 Corinthians 12, what does Paul say about one gift being more important than another?

4. How should we view each gift? Can you think of an obvious gift that would be clearly missing if no one used it in the church? What about a less obvious gift—how would we know that was missing if no one did it?

think FOR YOURSELF

Take a moment to thank God for making you on purpose, for a purpose, with just the right gifts to fulfill that purpose. Write down how you think your gift can help the body of Christ (the church) fit together and work as one body. If you are unclear about your spiritual gift, ask God to show you what your unique part of helping the church is. You may also want to ask your group or youth leader for insight into how God might have gifted you the next time you meet.

experience IT YOURSELF

Draw a large puzzle piece on a piece of paper and cut it out (or simply use an actual puzzle piece). On one side write both your name and your spiritual gift (if you know what it is). Put the puzzle piece in your gift box (you'll need it later). Let this represent your "piece" or role in the body of Christ. Thank God for giving you a part to play and ask him to use you to serve the church.

Devotion Three

d³   The Right Attitude

Last weekend, I had to help out at my church's Sunday school for little kids. I totally didn't want to help, but my youth pastor begged me to. The whole time I was frustrated with my youth pastor for talking me into it. But then I remembered that God asks us to serve, and that by serving others we actually please God. Just remembering that my serving was bigger than myself, that it was what God desired of me, helped me have a better attitude about it. I felt really good inside and actually was glad that I had helped out when it was over!

—Jade, 14

see FOR YOURSELF

Highlight or underline these verses in your Bible:

ask YOURSELF

1. Why is love so important for the proper functioning of spiritual gifts?

>> **ephesians 4:16**
Under his direction, the whole body is fitted together perfectly. As each part does its own special work, it helps the other parts grow, so that the whole body is healthy and growing and full of love.

>> **1 corinthians 13:3**
If I didn't love others, I would be of no value whatsoever.

>> **ephesians 6:7** (TNIV)
Serve wholeheartedly, as if you were serving the Lord, not people because you know that the Lord will reward each one of you for whatever good you do, whether you are slave or free.

2. How does knowing that God will reward you, and that you are serving God not people, make a difference in your attitude?

3. Having certain gifts does not mean that we should not serve in ways that all believers need to. What are some ways that we are all to serve, regardless of our gifts?

4. How does having a loving attitude change how you express your spiritual gifts? If you served others like Christ served you, what would change in the way you serve?

5. How is your attitude when it comes to serving others?

| 1 | 2 | 3 | 4 | 5 | 6 | 7 | 8 | 9 | 10 |

Let someone
else do it

Okay, if I have to

I really love
serving others

(**think** FOR YOURSELF)

What needs to change for you to have a more Christlike attitude when it comes to serving? Write down a few examples such as remembering that you are serving God, remembering the difference you are making by doing your part, or remembering that no matter how small or large your service is, it's important to God. Ask God to keep you focused on these truths while you are serving.

experience IT YOURSELF

Write "love" on an index card. Beneath the word write: "S − L = 0." This equation represents the truth that *Service* minus *Love* equals *zero*. Put this card in your gift box. Then pray, asking God to give you an attitude of love. Tomorrow look for opportunities to serve with the right attitude.

$S - L = 0$

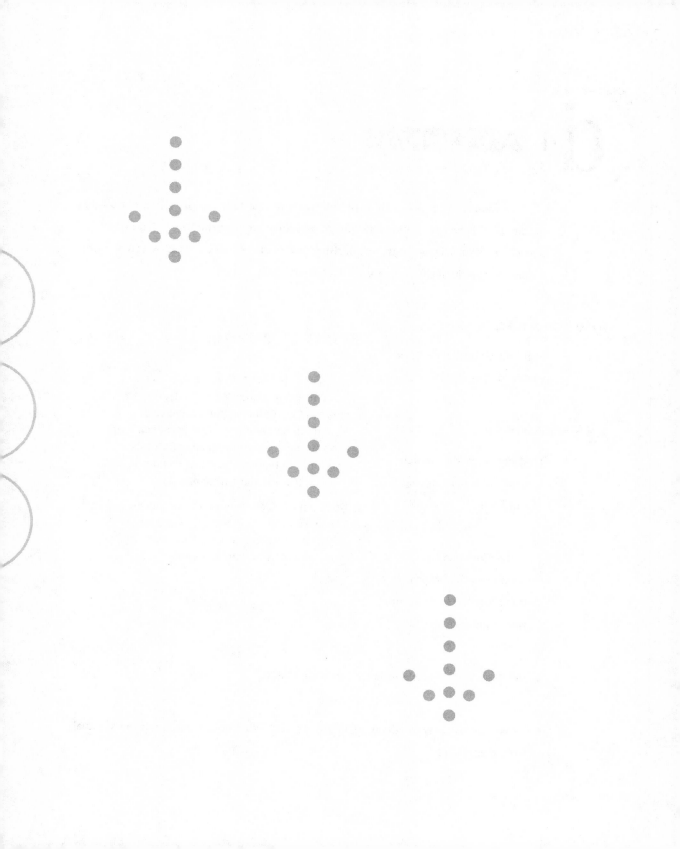

Devotion Four

d4   The Right Vine

God wants us to produce spiritual fruit (good works). Our spiritual gifts are tools that enable us to bear fruit. Ultimately, though, we don't produce the fruit—God does. For our gifts to bear fruit, we must be nourished in Christ. Without Christ, we can do nothing and our spiritual gifts will not produce lasting fruit.

s e e FOR YOURSELF

Highlight or underline these verses in your Bible:

a s k YOURSELF

1. What does the branch need in order to bear fruit? Why?

> **>> john 15:1, 4–5**
> [Jesus speaking] "I am the true vine, and my Father is the gardener. . . . Remain in me, and I will remain in you. For a branch cannot produce fruit if it is severed from the vine, and you cannot be fruitful apart from me.
>
> "Yes, I am the vine; you are the branches. *Those who remain in me, and I in them, will produce much fruit. For apart from me you can do nothing.*"

2. In the Christian life, what does the branch stand for? What does the vine stand for?

3. What do you think it means to "remain in Christ"?

4. What does this say to you as a Christ-follower? What does it say about the spiritual fruit in your life?

Are you a healthy branch that is bearing much fruit? One way to measure "fruitfulness" is to think about Paul's list of the fruit of the Spirit in Galatians 5:22–23 (see below). Use the continuums below to make an honest assessment of your spiritual fruitfulness while you were serving during this past month. Try to think of specific actions or situations on which to base your evaluation rather than just guessing. Circle the number on each continuum that best describes your response.

LOVE

How tender was your heart toward God and those you've served?

FADING   GROWING

1   2   3   4   5

JOY

Did your service bring you joy or did it feel like an obligation?

FADING   GROWING

1   2   3   4   5

PEACE

How content were you with your gifts and place of service?

FADING   GROWING

1   2   3   4   5

PATIENCE

How gracious and flexible were you when serving did not go the way you planned?

FADING   GROWING

1   2   3   4   5

KINDNESS

How often did you encourage and affirm others?

FADING   GROWING

| 1 | 2 | 3 | 4 | 5 |

GOODNESS

Did you find yourself doing the bare minimum or going the extra mile?

FADING   GROWING

| 1 | 2 | 3 | 4 | 5 |

FAITHFULNESS

Did you follow through on everything you said you would do?

FADING   GROWING

| 1 | 2 | 3 | 4 | 5 |

GENTLENESS

Were you willing to make time when someone needed a comforting word or a listening ear?

FADING   GROWING

| 1 | 2 | 3 | 4 | 5 |

SELF-CONTROL

Were you able to maintain an overall serving attitude when you felt strong impulses not to?

FADING   GROWING

| 1 | 2 | 3 | 4 | 5 |

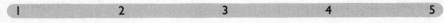

Write down on an index card one or two fruits of the Spirit you want God's help with. Put the card in your gift box. Ask God to help you have the attitudes reflected in the fruit of the Spirit, and to give you extra help in one or two areas you assessed as "fading." Tomorrow, ask God to help you put into practice the areas you want him to help you grow in. Remember, God desires for you to bear much fruit.

d⁵ The Church—The Hope of the World

When we use our spiritual gifts with an attitude of servanthood, a wonderful transformation takes place in us and through us. Our pride is broken, our attitudes become positive, and our ordinary lives become exciting adventures filled with hope and celebration. It starts today with the right vision and the right plan for you to be used by God to build the kingdom. Being used by God can be one of the most fulfilling experiences of your life!

see FOR YOURSELF

Highlight or underline these verses in your Bible:

ask YOURSELF

1. A cornerstone refers to the piece that completes a building and binds it all together. How is Christ the cornerstone to the church?

>> **ephesians 2:20–21**

We are his house, built on the foundation of the apostles and the prophets. And the cornerstone is Christ Jesus himself. *We who believe are carefully joined together, becoming a holy temple for the Lord.*

>> **matthew 25:21**

[In a parable, Jesus says,] "The master was full of praise. '*Well done, my good and faithful servant.* You have been faithful in handling this small amount, so now I will give you many more responsibilities. Let's celebrate together!'"

2. What does Jesus' parable from Matthew 25 say about how we should approach all our tasks, even the small ones?

3. In Matthew 25, why do you think the master wanted the servant to be faithful in the "small amount" before he gave him more responsibilities?

think FOR YOURSELF

What are you doing right now that is making a difference for God? List the steps you need to take to be more involved in your youth ministry or in your church. Ask God to help you be faithful in the small and big things so you can be a part of his work for your generation as he impacts the world through young, faithful people just like you.

experience IT YOURSELF

Find the puzzle piece you placed in your gift box a few days ago. Write on the back of it these words from Matthew 25: "Well done, my faithful child _____," and fill in your name. Place it back in the gift box. Spend time in prayer, thanking God that he wants to use you; that he has equipped you; that he has gifted you; that he has called you; that he has forgiven you; and that he has prepared a plan for your life. Let God know you desire to hear him speak the words, "Well done, my faithful child." Ask God to use you and the spiritual gifts he has given you to help others to build an Acts 2 church.

Open your gift box and look through all the different things you've learned. Pause at different moments to thank God for these realizations. Bring the box to the group study next week and share what your experience has been.

GROUP TEN

g10

Good Stewardship

Part 1: Show Me the Money

(**week** IN REVIEW)

1. Describe for the rest of the group the richest insight you had from your Daily Devotions.

2. Describe the most meaningful activity you did.

3. Pick one item from your gift box that was a meaningful learning experience for you. Explain why.

4. What other truths did you discover as you went through the contents of your gift box?

5. What questions or concerns were raised by your Daily Devotions?

opening UP

Frank was a young man from a wealthy family. But one day he heard a calling from God to pursue ministry, so he started selling some of his father's possessions to raise money for the work. Well, his father did not agree with Frank's calling and wanted the money back. He took Frank before a judge and the judge sided with the father. When this happened, Frank gave his father everything he owned. In fact, he even gave his father the clothes on his back and left the court naked. As he gave his clothes to his father, Frank said, "I will no longer call you my father; my Father in heaven will be my only father."

So began the ministry of Frank, whom we now call Saint Francis of Assisi (Assisi is a city in Italy). In the early part of the thirteenth century, Francis went on to lead one of the most profound renewal movements in the history of the church, radically depending on God to meet his every need and vowing not to own anything. He is an inspiring example of the freedom God gives us. He was also a great example of someone who realized that everything he had was God's. He acted as a trustee of all God had given him.

When we became followers of Christ, we received forgiveness from our sin (Grace) and freedom from being mastered by sin—meaning God is the leader of our lives. Following Jesus means allowing God to be the leader of our lives so that sin and selfishness no longer control us. God's Word asks us, "If God is for us, who can ever be against us?" (Romans 8:31). As followers of Jesus we enjoy the incredible freedom to live a life that is no longer conformed to this world, but a life that is totally transformed by God (Romans 12:1–2). This is what Growth is all about. God has given us special abilities (Gifts) to build the church, and to equip and love others in a supportive community (Groups) for accountability and encouragement. The last G we explore is about how we carry out our roles of being God's agents of blessings in the world. God wants us to be "good stewards." A steward is a caretaker, someone hired to manage another's property, finances, or affairs. The Lord of the Universe has chosen us to help manage his affairs.

1. When you hear the statement that God has set you free, what kind of freedom do you think about?

2. Have you sensed this freedom in your life? Why or why not?

3. What messages have you heard from the world about money and possessions? For instance, what have you heard about how important it is to make a lot of money so you can have all the "right" things to be happy and content? As you read the passages below, think about how messages from the world line up with God's truth about peace and contentment.

>>
psalm 145:14–16

The LORD helps the fallen and lifts up those bent beneath their loads.

All eyes look to you for help; you give them their food as they need it.

When you open your hand, you satisfy the hunger and thirst of every living thing.

>> ## matthew 6:32–34

[Jesus speaking] "Your heavenly Father already knows all your needs, and he will give you all you need from day to day if you live for him and make the Kingdom of God your primary concern.

"So don't worry about tomorrow, for tomorrow will bring its own worries. Today's trouble is enough for today."

read TOGETHER

Read Psalm 145:14–16 and Matthew 6:32–34.

explore TOGETHER

1. According to these passages, how involved is God in providing our everyday needs?

2. In what ways do you think God has provided what you need today?

3. Why does Jesus tell us not to worry about tomorrow?

4. What does it feel like to know God will meet all your daily needs? In what ways does this give you freedom? What kinds of things make it hard for you to really believe this is true?

experience IT TOGETHER

Living a life of freedom and trusting God as leader means realizing that everything we've been given is a gift from God. We don't own it—God does. On your own, look at the continuums below and assess where you are on each one. After you're done, get together with two or three people and share your findings.

| 1 | 2 | 3 | 4 | 5 | 6 | 7 | 8 | 9 | 10 |

My money is mine   My money is God's

| 1 | 2 | 3 | 4 | 5 | 6 | 7 | 8 | 9 | 10 |

My possessions are mine   My possessions are God's

| 1 | 2 | 3 | 4 | 5 | 6 | 7 | 8 | 9 | 10 |

My body is mine   My body is God's

| 1 | 2 | 3 | 4 | 5 | 6 | 7 | 8 | 9 | 10 |

My time is mine   My time is God's

| 1 | 2 | 3 | 4 | 5 | 6 | 7 | 8 | 9 | 10 |

My talents are mine   My talents are God's

Share with the group the times when it is difficult for you to trust God and why. Close in prayer, having each person individually list the area(s) in which they have difficulty really trusting God. Pray together to ask God to teach you in the next few weeks to be a good steward of all he has given you.

SESSION TEN

S¹⁰

Good Stewardship

Part 1: Show Me the Money

During the next two studies, we will look at how to honor God by being a good steward in every area of life: money, possessions, time, talents, and our bodies. This is the next step in the adventure in understanding spiritual transformation.

Devotion One

d 1

Whose Money Is It?

TV shows, ads, billboards, commercials all bombard us with the message that money is what it's all about. We may even begin to believe that if only we had a lot of money, we'd be happy. There is nothing wrong with having money; the problem comes when money becomes our master. God knew it could cause problems in our daily lives. It's a topic he talks a lot about in the Bible. God's view on money is what we'll look at this week. Now is the time in your life to start thinking about and understanding the importance of stewardship.

see FOR YOURSELF

Highlight or underline these verses in your Bible. Then circle two words in each passage that remind you of what you need to work on.

>> **leviticus 27:30**
A *tenth of the produce of the land,* whether grain or fruit, *belongs to the* Lord and must be set apart to him as holy.

>> **proverbs 3:9**
Honor the Lord *with your wealth* and with the best part of everything your land produces.

>> **acts 20:35**
I [Paul] have been a constant example of how you can help the poor by working hard. You should remember the words of the Lord Jesus: *"It is more blessed to give than to receive."*

ask YOURSELF

1. Accoding to Leviticus 27:30, why do you think God asks for 10 percent and allows us to keep 90 percent? What does this say about God's generosity?

2. According to Proverbs 3:9, what does it mean to *honor* someone? How does giving money to God's work honor him?

3. According to Acts 20:35, in what ways is it more blessed to give than to receive? Can you think of a time when you really felt blessed by giving something to someone?

think FOR YOURSELF

Regardless of whether you have a lot of money or very little, it is important to learn how to handle appropriately whatever God has given you. And now is a good time to really grasp God's views on money in order to battle the "gimme more" attitude our culture encourages. The More Monster starts early in our lives, but it's important to understand now that it will never satisfy your soul.

Think for a moment about how you've been influenced by the world to believe that money will bring true happiness. In the space below, write out a brief prayer asking God to give you wisdom and discernment to never buy the enemy's lies about money. Ask God to help you be content and to trust him alone for meeting your needs.

experience IT YOURSELF

Once again, God says it is more blessed to give than to receive. Think of at least one way you can be a giver tomorrow at school, instead of just a receiver. See what opportunities God provides for you.

Devotion Two

d² Debt Free

Have you ever found yourself saying things like "I *need* a new computer" or "I *need* those shoes." There's a big difference between a *want* and a *need*. You don't *need* a new computer or shoes—you *want* those things. What you *need* is food, water, and air. When we think of our *wants* as *needs,* we start thinking we deserve them, or even that we are owed them. Instead of gratitude for having our *needs* fulfilled, we focus on getting our *wants* met and so we stop saying "thank you."

There's nothing wrong with having wants, but if we don't know the difference between *wants* and *needs* now, it could someday lead to being controlled by our wants. This is why some people get into debt, because they will do whatever it takes to get what they want *right now.* They spend money they don't have, which is what we call "debt." *Debt* is when we owe someone money. It occurs when we buy something now but pay for it later. The problem comes when people want too many things now—a big house, a new stereo, a big TV, and so on—and accumulate so much debt that their lives become controlled by what they owe. They become prisoners of their possessions. This has become a huge problem for many adults, who end up working all their lives to try to get out of debt. That's why it is so important for you to learn at an early age about the wisdom God gives us when it comes to our money.

see FOR YOURSELF

Highlight or underline these verses in your Bible:

>> **romans 13:8**
Pay all your debts, except the debt of love for others. You can never finish paying that!

>> **hebrews 13:5**
Stay away from the love of money; be satisfied with what you have. For God has said, "I will never fail you. I will never forsake you."

>> **1 timothy 6:17**

Tell those who are rich in this world not to be proud and not to trust in their money, which will soon be gone. But their trust should be in the living God, who richly gives us all we need for our enjoyment.

1. According to Romans 13:8, what is the only debt we should have?

2. What do you think it means to trust in God and not in money? Have you seen examples of people who "trust in their money"? How does trusting first in God change how we deal with our *wants?*

3. According to 1 Timothy 6:17, why does God "richly give us all we need"?

t h i n k FOR YOURSELF

Write below all the things you need or want right now. What have you been dreaming about, asking for, or craving? It can be things, events, relationships, etc.

On your list above, circle those things you literally could not live without. These are your basic needs. Now cross off those things that would not really impact your life if you did not get them. These are your wants. (Wants are not bad or unimportant; the point is not to treat them as needs if they are really wants.) If there is anything left, try to label it as a need or a want depending on how much your life would be diminished by not receiving it. Once you have distinguished your needs from your wants, reflect on how you think of these things differently than you did before this exercise. Does it make any difference to see your desires in this way? Why or why not?

experience IT YOURSELF

Ask a few adults in your family—parents, grandparents, aunts, uncles, etc.—about debt and what advice they have for you about saving and spending. Let them know you want to honor God with all he has given you. Ask if they have experienced God's blessing in areas of giving.

Devotion Three

d³

Living Large

We constantly receive the message that we are to "live large" by having more: a bigger TV, a new car, a nicer home, expensive jewelry. This triggers our discontentment and causes us to become critical and unsatisfied with what we do have. We start telling ourselves that our things don't measure up: *Our car is too old,* or, *I wish we lived in a bigger house.* God's Word warns us about that trap and the harmful effects of desiring money.

s e e FOR YOURSELF

Highlight or underline these verses in your Bible:

>> **1 timothy 6:9–10**

People who long to be rich fall into temptation and are trapped by many foolish and harmful desires that plunge them into ruin and destruction. *For the love of money is at the root of all kinds of evil.* And some people, craving money, have wandered from the faith and pierced themselves with many sorrows.

>> **philippians 4:12–13, 19**

I know how to live on almost nothing or with everything. I have learned the secret of living in every situation, whether it is with a full stomach or empty, with plenty or little. For I can do everything with the help of Christ who gives me the strength I need. . . .

And this same God who takes care of me will supply all your needs from his glorious riches, which have been given to us in Christ Jesus.

a s k YOURSELF

1. According to 1 Timothy 6, what is the danger of wanting to be rich?

2. Lots of people think this verse says money itself is the root of evil—but that's *not* what it says! What is at the root of all evil?

3. Why do you think longing for money can cause people to "wander from the faith"?

4. According to Philippians 4 above, who can, and will, meet our needs for our lifetime?

5. What is Paul's secret in Philippians 4 for how to live in any situation?

6. What would Paul say is a healthy view of money?

think FOR YOURSELF

Paul, in Philippians 4:12, says he has learned to be content with what he has, whether little or much. How content are you with what God has provided you with? In the space below, write a brief letter to God thanking him for what you have. Ask him to give you a heart of contentment and keep you from desiring more or comparing yourself and your situation to others.

experience IT YOURSELF

How long has it been since you told your mom or dad how thankful you are for the things they provide for you? Write a note, thanking them and—if needed—asking for their forgiveness for having the wrong attitude. Ask God to give you the right words to write this note, then thank him for your parents and all their provisions.

d4   Being a Cheerful Giver

Devotion Four

God does not want us to give because we have to. He looks at our hearts. He wants to see an attitude of joy and compassion in our giving. When we give that way, God gives back to us more in many, many ways. It is like a dad who sees his child sharing his toys or food. That dad wants to give his child more because he is proud of the child's generous heart. How much more will God give to us when he sees our giving hearts.

see FOR YOURSELF

Highlight or underline these verses in your Bible from the apostle Paul:

ask YOURSELF

1. How is giving like farmers planting seed? What is the crop in Paul's analogy?

>> **2 corinthians 9:6–8**
Remember this—a farmer who plants only a few seeds will get a small crop. But the one who plants generously will get a generous crop. You must each make up your own mind as to how much you should give. *Don't give reluctantly or in response to pressure. For God loves the person who gives cheerfully.* And God will generously provide all you need. Then you will always have everything you need and plenty left over to share with others.

>> **2 corinthians 8:11–12**
Give whatever you can according to what you have. *If you are really eager to give, it isn't important how much you are able to give.* God wants you to give what you have, not what you don't have.

2. What does God look for when we give and why?

3. How does God repay a cheerful giver?

4. If the amount of the gift is not important to God, what is important to him?

5. What is the best motivation for giving?

Using the three continuums below, assess yourself. Circle the number that best describes your response.

1. What is the general condition of your heart when it comes to giving your money or helping someone?

| 1 | 2 | 3 | 4 | 5 | 6 | 7 | 8 | 9 | 10 |

Reluctant Heart   Cheerful heart

2. Think back to the last time you bought a gift for someone (using your own money). Measure the feeling in your heart.

| 1 | 2 | 3 | 4 | 5 | 6 | 7 | 8 | 9 | 10 |

Reluctant Heart   Cheerful heart

3. Recall the last time you donated money to a ministry or church. Measure the feeling in your heart. (Be honest!)

| 1 | 2 | 3 | 4 | 5 | 6 | 7 | 8 | 9 | 10 |

Reluctant Heart   Cheerful heart

Look back over your answers above and reflect on your responses. Ask God to give you the cheerful heart of a giver.

experience IT YOURSELF

Be quiet and still. Ask God to show you the needs he wants you to meet in the people around you. It may be as simple as buying someone lunch, or taking them to a movie, or giving to the local church that runs a soup kitchen to feed the poor. See who comes to mind as you are quiet before God. Ask God to help you give with a cheerful heart!

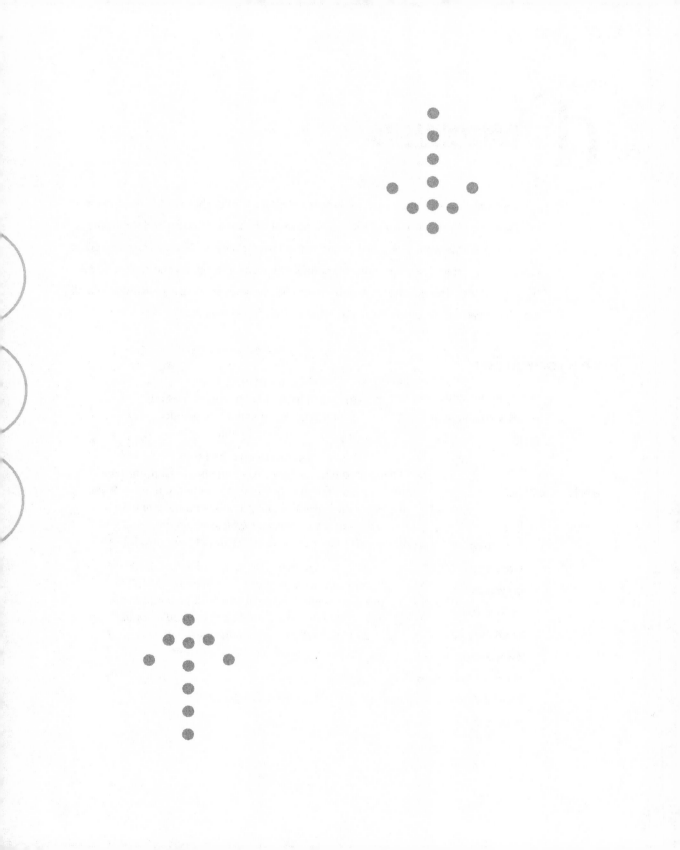

Devotion Five

d5   The Blessing

God makes it very clear that he wants to bless his faithful children. He doesn't mean *faithful* as in "super Christians." He means normal Christians like you and me trying to live by the truths we are learning about in the Five Gs: Grace, Growth, Groups, Gifts, Good Stewardship. Christians who are faithful in the small things get the chance to take on larger things. The question is, whether with big things or small, are we faithful with all God has given us? Today we'll see just what this blessing looks like.

see FOR YOURSELF

Highlight or underline these verses in your Bible:

ask YOURSELF

1. If you own something, what rights do you expect to have about the thing you own? According to Psalm 24, what does God own? If God wants to bless us, what is at his disposal?

>> **psalm 24:1**
The earth is the LORD's, and everything in it. The world and all its people belong to him.

>> **malachi 3:10**
"Bring all the tithes [offerings and gifts to God] into the storehouse so there will be enough food in my Temple. If you do," says the LORD Almighty, "I will open the windows of heaven for you. *I will pour out a blessing so great you won't have enough room to take it in!* Try it! Let me prove it to you!"

>> **matthew 25:21**
[Jesus is telling a parable] "The master was full of praise. 'Well done, my good and faithful servant. *You have been faithful in handling this small amount, so now I will give you many more responsibilities.* Let's celebrate together!'"

2. According to Malachi, to what extent does God want to bless us?

3. How does God want to reward our faithfulness? What jobs has God given us to do that he expects us to be faithful in?

think FOR YOURSELF

God wants to bless your life. He has made a promise personally to you. Now think about that for a moment. The God of the universe wants to bless your life—how awesome is that! All he wants you to do is honor and trust him with what he's given you by giving back a portion to him. In the space below, write a prayer telling God you want to honor and trust him with your money now and for a lifetime. Thank him in advance for his blessing on your life.

experience IT YOURSELF

Take out a dollar bill, and let it represent all the money you'll ever receive in your life. Take a pencil and write in the corner of the dollar, "It is yours." Then put it on your mirror. When you see the words, "It is yours," remember that all we have is God's, including our money. Look at yourself in the mirror and remember that God wants to pour out a blessing on your life.

g 11 Good Stewardship

Part 2: All I Have Is Yours, God

1. Describe for the rest of the group the richest insight you had from your Daily Devotions.

2. Describe the most meaningful activity you did.

3. What did you discover as you gave a gift to someone?

4. What questions or concerns were raised by your Daily Devotions?

opening UP

I was sitting with some of my friends after the worship service. The pastor was nearby and leaned over to me and said, "You have an awesome voice. It would be great if you'd think about joining the worship team." At first I thought she was just being nice, but she really meant it. It has been great being able to help lead people in worship. I love it!

—*Mary, 15*

We were having a small group Bible study when one of the guys challenged us about how much time we spend online. He said he had been thinking how much time he had been wasting. The more we talked, I realized I had been wasting a lot of time too. So we promised each other that we would "donate" some of the time we had been spending on the computer and spend it for God—either reading a devotional book or Scripture, praying, or helping people. My relationship with God really grew after that.

—*Matt, 13*

My friend Jon challenged me to start running with him in the mornings to get in shape. I hated running but I liked spending time with Jon. Since we've been doing that for a while now, it's getting easier. I'm even feeling more energy throughout the day. Mom thinks I've lost weight (maybe), but I do know I feel better.

—*Gary, 17*

God has made you for his glory. He promises that he'll finish his good work in you and allow you to become a fully devoted follower of Christ. Our part is becoming a good steward (manager) of all God has given us. This includes not only our money but also our talents, time, and bodies. God has given us many gifts. It's up to us to give back to him what he's already given us.

1. God has given you talents. Some of them you may not have even discovered yet—other talents you are in the process of discovering. For the talents you know you have now, what are you doing to develop your talents to honor God?

2. If you had to evaluate your overall use of time, how would you rate yourself?

1	2	3	4	5	6	7	8	9	10

I do not manage my time at all

I try to use my time wisely

I have balance and effectiveness with my time

3. Explain why you gave yourself the mark you did.

4. Physical health is an area we have to steward well. In what ways could you care for your body to show it is a valuable gift from God?

>> **philippians 1:6**
I am sure that God, who began the good work within you, will continue his work until it is finally finished on that day when Christ Jesus comes back again.

>> **1 timothy 4:12**
Don't let anyone think less of you because you are young. Be an example to all believers in what you teach, in the way you live, in your love, your faith, and your purity.

read TOGETHER

Read Philippians 1:6 and 1 Timothy 4:12.

explore TOGETHER

1. What is the "good work" God began in you?

2. How does knowing God will finish what he's begun in our lives motivate and encourage us to give him our all?

3. Does he expect us to do it by human strength? Why or why not?

4. Can you tell if you are becoming more like Christ since God began his work in you? Explain what you have noticed.

5. What are all the ways we are to be an example to others, according to Paul in 1 Timothy 4:12? What role does being young play in whether or not we are a good example to others?

experience IT TOGETHER

Distribute index cards to everyone in the group and complete this activity individually. Write "All of me" on the card. Spend a few minutes in prayer, thanking God for making you his workmanship. Ask yourself if you are willing to say this prayer: "Lord, I am willing to give you all of me" (meaning complete ownership of all he has given you). If you are willing, then sign the index card. Close your time in prayer, letting God know what this means to you. Keep the card with you when you get back together for Community Time.

community TIME

Gather back together in a circle. One at a time, go around the group and place your card in the middle of the circle. As you do so, say, "Lord, I give you all of me." If you did not feel ready to sign the card, briefly tell the group what's keeping you from feeling ready. Close in prayer, having each person express gratitude for what God is doing in his or her life.

SESSION ELEVEN

S 11

Good Stewardship

Part 2: All I Have Is Yours, God

The next study of good stewardship focuses on how to have an attitude that says, "Everything I have is yours, God—not only my money but also my time, my possessions, my body, and my talents. It's all yours, God."

Devotion One

d 1   Having More Than I Need

Have you ever looked in your closet and said, "I have nothing to wear"? Have you ever looked at a full refrigerator or pantry and declared, "There's nothing here to eat"? One student confessed, "I ran out of the house, jumped into my car, threw in my new CD, took off down the street, and realized I forgot my cell phone. I said to myself, *I can't go anywhere without my cell phone!*" Our lives are filled with a lot of "stuff"—gadgets, electronics—much more than we'll ever need. God wants us to enjoy life, but he also wants us not to forget those who are less fortunate. He wants us to remember to give thanks and be good stewards of the abundance he has given us.

see FOR YOURSELF

Highlight or underline these verses in your Bible:

>> **proverbs 21:2–3**

People may think they are doing what is right, *but the Lord examines the heart.*

The Lord is more pleased when we do what is just and right than when we give him sacrifices.

>> **1 john 3:17–18**

But if anyone has enough money to live well and sees a brother or sister in need and refuses to help—how can God's love be in that person?

Dear children, *let us stop just saying we love each other;* let us really show it by our actions.

>> **luke 12:15, 21**

Then [Jesus] said, "Beware! Don't be greedy for what you don't have. *Real life is not measured by how much we own. . . .*

"Yes, a person is a fool to store up earthly wealth but not have a rich relationship with God."

1. According to Proverbs 21, what is the problem if we merely *think* what we are doing is right? According to God, what makes our actions *really* right? What are some examples you may know of where people did things they thought were right but were not?

2. What does it tell us about God that he prefers "what is just and right" to receiving sacrifices?

3. What is the measure of whether we love someone, according to 1 John 3?

4. How does this affect how we should act when we see people in need?

5. Define *greed* in your own words. As a Christ-follower, how do you handle greed?

6. In Luke 12, why does Jesus call a person a fool for wanting to have wealth over a rich relationship with God?

think FOR YOURSELF

Write down an inventory of all your possessions. Stop, look around, and consider *everything* you own: TV, computer, clothes, shoes, stereo, games, books, CDs, maybe a car. Be specific: seven pair of shoes, six sweaters, one stereo, etc. The point of this exercise is to get you in touch with how much stuff surrounds you. Could Paul's warning about the love of money (1 Timothy 6:10) apply to you? Ask yourself, *Does God own my possessions? Do*

I take care of them like they were his? If they were taken away, would I trust that God is in control? In the space below, write a prayer asking God to help you be a good steward of all you have. Ask him to give you a thankful heart.

experience IT YOURSELF

Consider what you own from God's perspective. Are there things you don't really need that others could use? Identify some items you can either give to someone in need or donate to a charity. Talk to your parents about your willingness to help others, then together come up with a plan of what you can do.

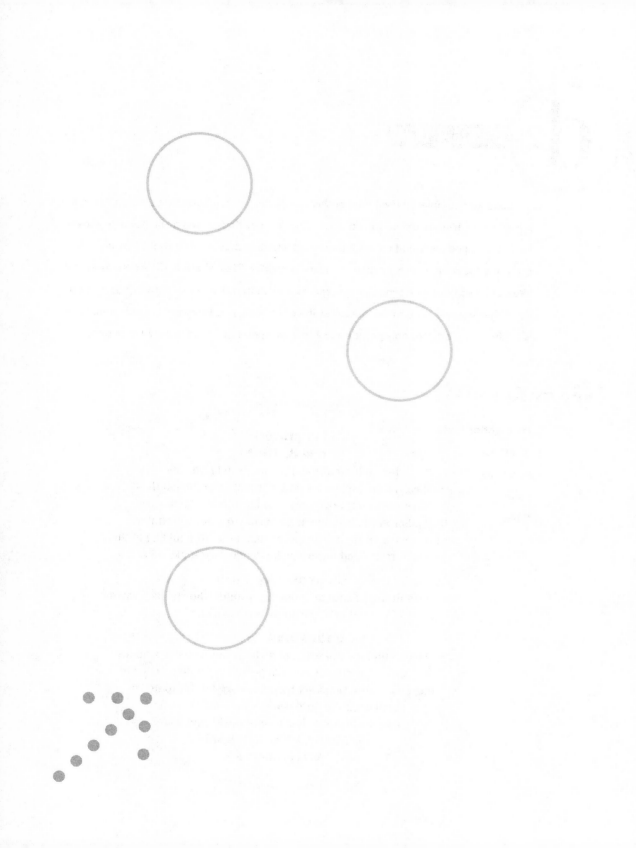

Time Out

Devotion Two

Luke just completed level four on his computer game; it took three hours. Next he talked to his friends online for an hour. Then he decided to watch his favorite movie. Finally, he called his friend to see if there was anything they wanted to do that night. We can put a lot of time into fun and mundane activities. Then there is the other extreme: We can be so busy with school, work, sports, and church that we run out of hours in our day. Either way, we need to ask ourselves if we are being good stewards of our time. Time is a gift from God. We only get it once. How we spend our time is very important.

see FOR YOURSELF

Highlight or underline these verses in your Bible:

>> **proverbs 6:6–8, 10–11**
Take a lesson from the ants, you lazybones. Learn from their ways and be wise! Even though they have no prince, governor, or ruler to make them work, they labor hard all summer, gathering food for the winter. . . . A little extra sleep, a little more slumber, a little folding of the hands to rest—and poverty will pounce on you like a bandit.

>> **proverbs 10:5**
A wise youth works hard all summer; a youth who sleeps away the hour of opportunity brings shame.

>> **ephesians 5:15–18**
So be careful how you live, not as fools but as those who are wise. Make the most of every opportunity for doing good in these evil days. Don't act thoughtlessly, but try to understand what the Lord wants you to do. Don't be drunk with wine, because that will ruin your life. Instead, let the Holy Spirit fill and control you.

1. According to Proverbs 6, in what ways should we imitate ants? What is the significance of their working so hard even without a ruler or governor?

2. According to Proverbs 10, why do you think poverty comes upon the one who sleeps too much?

3. What do the verses from Proverbs tell us about how we should use our time?

4. Contrast the two ways to live Paul describes in Ephesians 5. What does he recommend and what does he warn us about?

Think back and review your last three days. Use the chart on the next page to identify how you used your time, including time for sleep and rest. Be as detailed as possible.

Try to add up the hours you spent on fun activities; on work or study; in service to the church or to others; with friends or family; in sports or exercise; sleeping. Do any of the totals surprise you? Are there things you would do differently now that you see how your time was used? As you look over the chart, how would you rate yourself as a steward of the time God has given you?

What are two decisions you need to make in order to be a better steward of your time? How could you make better use of your time by rearranging some of your activities?

TIME	DAY ONE	DAY TWO	DAY THREE
6:00 A.M.			
7:00 A.M.			
8:00 A.M.			
9:00 A.M.			
10:00 A.M.			
11:00 A.M.			
12:00 noon			
1:00 P.M.			
2:00 P.M.			
3:00 P.M.			
4:00 P.M.			
5:00 P.M.			
6:00 P.M.			
7:00 P.M.			
8:00 P.M.			
9:00 P.M.			
10:00 P.M.			
11:00 P.M.			
12:00 midnight			
1:00 A.M.			
2:00 A.M.			
3:00 A.M.			
4:00 A.M.			
5:00 A.M.			

In the space below, list two or three projects or tasks you've been meaning to get to but have been avoiding. Set a date to complete each one. Now decide how you will find the time to reach your goal (for example, one hour after dinner for the next five days).

Next, write the following phrase in big letters on a piece of paper: "24 Hours/7 Days a Week." God gives us a gift each day of twenty-four hours, and you know that time with God is essential for a Christ-follower. How much time do you want to give back to him this week. For example, spending time in prayer, Bible study, worship, service. Write down how many minutes you will give back to God next to the "24 Hours/7 Days a Week" on the paper. Now look at the time you have for yourself. Is it too much to give back to God? We are told to love God and to love others. When you think about how you spend the time you have for yourself, are you focusing on people or things? Spend a few moments thanking God for your time, and tell yourself that you will use this gift wisely.

Devotion Three

d3   The Perfect Body

You can't go too long without seeing or hearing about how you need to be in shape, or have the perfect body. Most of the time, the reasons are not to honor God but to get the right boyfriend or girlfriend. God cares about how we take care of our bodies—not to please people but to honor God.

see FOR YOURSELF

Highlight or underline these verses in your Bible:

ask YOURSELF

1. Who owns your body? What do you think it means to see your body as a "temple of the Holy Spirit"?

>> **1 corinthians 6:19–20**
Don't you know that *your body is the temple of the Holy Spirit,* who lives in you and was given to you by God? *You do not belong to yourself,* for God bought you with a high price. So you must honor God with your body.

>> **1 timothy 4:8**
Physical exercise has some value, but spiritual exercise is much more important, for it promises a reward in both this life and the next.

2. According to 1 Corinthians 6, what are all the reasons Paul mentions in the passages above for why we should take care of our bodies?

3. According to 1 Timothy 4, how does Paul contrast the different priorities for spiritual and physical exercises? How much time during a typical week do you spend on each?

Think back on the last twenty-four hours and then respond to the questions below.

1. What have you eaten in the last twenty-four hours?

2. How many hours of sleep did you get?

3. How much time did you spend in exercise?

Do your answers reflect the fact that your body is a temple of the Holy Spirit? If some-one gave you a pet worth $1 million and said your job was to care for it, how would you treat your new pet? Now think about the price that was paid for your body? How should this change the way you take care of your body—what you eat, how you rest, how you exercise. Ask God to help you live a lifestyle of appropriate fitness, rest, and diet to honor him with your body. Be specific with what needs to be done and ask God to help you reach your goals.

It has been said that it takes twenty-one days to form a habit. In the space below, write down four goals you can achieve in the next twenty-one days to improve your body for God's service. It can be as simple as going for a walk in the evening each night, working out three days a week, eating right, going to bed on time, not drinking as much soda. Remember to set goals you can reach. After the twenty-one days are up, go twenty-one more days with two new goals. Again, remember to set goals you can reach each time. Start today. Pray and ask God to give you the willpower to be a good steward of your body.

Devotion Four

d4   Talented Humility

God has given each person different talent(s): singing, writing, athletic ability, drawing, cooking, mechanical skill. Some of these talents you may know now, others you may discover later on in life. The talents God has given us are a way to bring blessing to God and to others, but they can also be a temptation to feel pride. Many people have fallen away from God by pursuing their talents for its own rewards and not in service to God. How we use these talents and how we develop them are part of good stewardship.

see FOR YOURSELF

Highlight or underline these verses in your Bible:

>> **genesis 1:27**
God created people *in his own image;* God patterned them after himself; male and female he created them.

>> **proverbs 16:18**
Pride goes before destruction, and haughtiness before a fall.

>> **1 peter 5:6–7**
So humble yourselves under the mighty power of God, and in his good time he will honor you. Give all your worries and cares to God, for he cares about what happens to you.

>>
psalm 34:1–5
I will praise the LORD at all times. I will constantly speak his praises. / *I will boast only in the LORD;* let all who are discouraged take heart. / Come, let us tell of the LORD's greatness; let us exalt his name together. / I prayed to the LORD, and he answered me, *freeing me from all my fears.* / Those who look to him for help will be radiant with joy; / no shadow of shame will darken their faces.

1. How does being made in the image of God guarantee us a talent?

2. According to 1 Peter 5, if we humble ourselves with the talents we have, what does God promise us? If we let pride take control of our talents, what will be the result?

3. Define *pride* in your own words. When does being proud of something turn into something opposed to God?

4. According to Proverbs 16, 1 Peter 5, and Psalm 34, what are some ways to stay humble rather than prideful?

5. How can you apply this advice to your life?

think FOR YOURSELF

We all have a talent or talents God has given us. What talents have you discovered so far in your life? Ask yourself if you have a prideful spirit about the talent you have. Write a letter to God below, thanking him for the talents you have and asking him to show you ways you can honor him with your talent. Then let him know you will give him the praise (and not yourself) for the ability he has given you when the opportunity arises to use your talent.

(**experience** IT YOURSELF)

Think of a way you can use your talent to bring blessing to others. Be prepared to give praise to God when you are asked. Right now, write down what you would say if a person was to give you a compliment about your talent. For example, "I couldn't do it without God." Or "I thank God for the talent he has given me." After writing it down, take a moment and say it out loud, offering the praise to God.

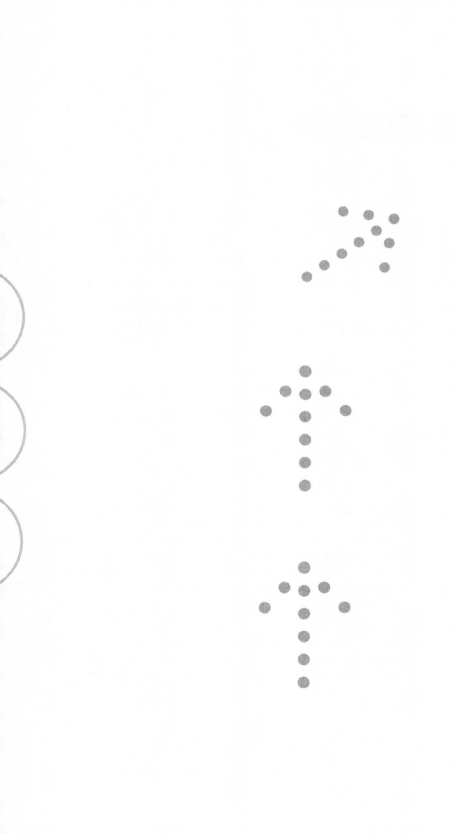

Devotion Five

d5

Being a Good Trustee

Have you ever heard the word *trustee*? A trustee is someone who has been given charge over possessions to take care of them. In other words, it has the same meaning as *steward*. In God's kingdom, being his trustee means letting God "own" all that is his: our money, our possessions, our bodies, our talents and gifts—including life itself. When we entrust God with full responsibility and leadership of our lives, we can expect to be given more opportunities to grow and serve, and experience spiritual transformation at its best. Giving God everything will take trust—but remember, God is trustworthy.

see FOR YOURSELF

Use a pen or pencil to draw a box around this long passage in your Bible. Then highlight or underline the verses that have the most meaning for you.

>> **matthew 25:14–29**

[Jesus speaking] "The Kingdom of Heaven can be illustrated by the story of a man going on a trip. He called together his servants and gave them money to invest for him while he was gone. He gave five bags of gold to one, two bags of gold to another, and one bag of gold to the last—dividing it in proportion to their abilities—and then left on his trip. The servant who received the five bags of gold began immediately to invest the money and soon doubled it. The servant with two bags of gold also went right to work and doubled the money. But the servant who received the one bag of gold dug a hole in the ground and hid the master's money for safekeeping.

"After a long time their master returned from his trip and called them to give an account of how they had used his money. The servant to whom he had entrusted the five bags of gold said, 'Sir, . . . I have doubled the amount.' The master was full of praise. *'Well done, my good and faithful servant. You have been faithful in handling this small amount, so now I will give you many more responsibilities. Let's celebrate together!'.* . .

[To the second servant he said,]
"'Well done, my good and . . .

(cont.)

. . . faithful servant. You have been faithful in handling this small amount, so now I will give you many more responsibilities. Let's celebrate together!'

"Then the servant with the one bag of gold came and said, 'Sir, I know you are a hard man, harvesting crops you didn't plant and gathering crops you didn't cultivate. I was afraid I would lose your money, so I hid it in the earth and here it is.'

"But the master replied, 'You wicked and lazy servant! You think I'm a hard man, do you, harvesting crops I didn't plant and gathering crops I didn't cultivate? Well, you should at least have put my money into the bank so I could have some interest. Take the money from this servant and give it to the one with the ten bags of gold. *To those who use well what they are given, even more will be given, and they will have an abundance. But from those who are unfaithful, even what little they have will be taken away.*'"

ask YOURSELF

1. What were the responses of the three servants to their jobs? What motivated the first two servants and what motivated the third?

2. What excuse does the third servant give for his actions? Why doesn't his excuse make sense? What was his attitude about what was entrusted to him?

3. How does the master reward the faithful servants? What do you think it would feel like to hear God say to you, "Well done, my good and faithful servant"?

4. Why did God take the gold from the third servant and give it to the one who had ten bags?

think FOR YOURSELF

Being a good steward starts with an attitude that says "everything I have is God's." If this is the attitude you desire, say a prayer out loud naming each of the areas in which God has given you the chance to be a good steward. After each item, say out loud to God, "It is all yours!"

Close in prayer, thanking God for giving it all back to you and allowing you to be a trustee of his property. Let him know you want to be a faithful

> My time—it is all yours, God.
>
> My possessions—they're yours, God.
>
> My money—it's yours, God.
>
> My body—it's yours, God.
>
> My talents— they are all yours, God.

experience IT FOR YOURSELF

In the last several weeks, we've been studying the characteristics of a fully devoted follower of Jesus. We've looked at ways we can put markers in our lives that will help us on our journey. These markers are the Five Gs—Grace, Growth, Groups, Gifts, Good Stewardship. Take a moment now and think about each of these areas in your life. This is a good way to check and see if you are on the right path, growing stronger and becoming more like Jesus. Make it a habit to check the markers a few times during the year to help you stay focused on your spiritual journey.

On the six continuums below, put an X on the spot that best describes where you are right now in your life. For each one, take a moment and thank God. Celebrate where you are so far in the journey.

GRACE FOR OTHERS

| I have no compassion for non-Christians | I think about evangelism sometimes | I have an Impact List and pray for my close friends that aren't Christ-followers | I have strong compassion and share my faith whenever God gives me an opportunity |

GRACE IN MY LIFE

I have not accepted God's gift of grace in my life	I have a hard time understanding how God could completely forgive me	I have accepted and am starting to understand God's amazing grace in my life	I have received and am thankful everyday for God's grace in my life

GROWTH

I am not growing in my relationship with God	I am making some progress	I am growing in my relationship and spiritual disciplines	I am committed and growing and have established spiritual disciplines in my life

GROUPS

I have no group life	I have a couple Christian friends	I am involved in a small group	I am in real community, growing and doing life together with my friends

GIFTS

I do not have spiritual gifts	I know I have gifts, but have not discovered or know much about them	I know I have gifts and am in the process of discovering what they are	I know my gifts and am using and developing them in serving God

GOOD STEWARDSHIP

|———|

I do not	I thank God	I give God thanks	I am becoming
acknowledge	sometimes for	all the time	a good, wise,
God for what	what I have	for what he's	and effective stew-
he's given me		given me	ard of what God
in my life			has given me

Now go back and put a star on each continuum to symbolize where you want to be one year from now. Then pray to God, asking him to show you the way to become more devoted to him. Remember Philippians 4:13: "For I can do everything with the help of Christ who gives me the strength I need."

"Thank you for making me so wonderfully complex! Your workmanship is marvelous—and how well I know it" (Psalm 139:14).

Congratulations! Great job! You have completed an incredible eleven-week spiritual journey that has given you markers—the Five Gs—to help you stay on course for a lifetime journey with God. This calls for a celebration!

King David knew how to celebrate. In Psalm 139 he praised and celebrated God when he realized he was wonderfully made in God's image. He knew God loved him, and that God's works—which included David—were wonderful. The same thing that was true for David is true for you today. *You* are God's beloved. He has given you grace; he has promised to continually help you grow on your spiritual journey; he has set you in community with others; he has gifted you to do wonderful kingdom work; and he has made you a trustee over all he has given you.

God is pleased that you have taken time in these last eleven weeks to become more like his Son, Jesus. Take time during the next week to look back over all you have learned and accomplished. Next time you meet with your small group, celebrate everything that has happened since you began this study. Thank your accountability partner this week by writing him or her a note or even buying a small gift. Thank your small group leaders and others who have helped you during this time. But most important, spend some time in prayer, thanking God for his amazing gift of love for you. Remember that you are wonderfully made and beloved by God.

Congratulations on completing the commitment you made to being a fully devoted follower of Christ!

afterword

g Leader's Notes

Spiritual transformation happens most effectively in the context of small groups. Small groups give students the opportunity to meet face-to-face, get questions answered, and share their own thoughts. Small groups also allow for accountability and encouragement—to live out the truths that are being learned.

The Group Study for each week helps students get ready for the five Daily Devotions that follow in which they will discover deeper truths about each of the Five Gs. The questions in each Group Study are designed to *promote discussion* rather than coming up with the one "right" answer.

The Group Studies are designed for small groups of three to ten students. If you have a larger group, you might consider breaking it up into two or more smaller groups. It's also recommended that at the beginning of the study each student find an accountability partner to encourage each other as they complete this course.

The study includes an introduction and in-depth treatment of the Five Gs—Grace, Growth, Groups, Gifts, Good Stewardship. Each G has two units—a unit consists of one Group Study and five Daily Devotions. The entire study, if done weekly, will take eleven weeks. If done every other week, it will take twenty-two weeks to complete.

Although the material in this book covers eleven weeks, it is highly recommended to allow twelve weeks so you can have a celebration gathering to mark the completion of the study. Use this gathering to affirm each student individually and to share how you've seen each student mature as a Christ-follower. Think of creative ways to celebrate—

perhaps writing each student a personal note, or having them share stories about their experiences during the last eleven weeks. Invite students to share how they've grown in community as well as in their personal relationship with God.

group STUDIES

Week in Review
At the beginning of each new study, review the questions by asking students what they have learned and experienced during the previous week.

Opening Up
This begins with a story that can be read out loud or read together silently. Wherever possible, real student stories are used. It is important for students to realize that they are not too young to be deeply challenged by God. The story is followed by an introduction to the week's topic and some general questions to stir up their thinking.

Read Together
Each Bible reference is printed in the study itself so you can all read the same Bible translation. However, it's best to also have students open their own Bibles and highlight the verses being studied. This gets them in the habit of highlighting verses during their devotions.

Explore/Discuss Together
The questions that follow the Bible readings are open-ended and do not always have a simple or obvious answer. It is important that students learn to treat Scripture with respect for its depth as a literary as well as inspired work. When appropriate, the context for a Bible verse is also provided. Be prepared for questions and issues that may not fit perfectly the topic outline. After some discussion, you can steer the discussion back to the topic at hand.

Experience It Together
Each Group Study contains an exercise designed to promote interaction or experimentation with the topic of the study.

Community Time
This is a closing prayer or exercise that sets up the students for individual Daily Devotions on the topic of the Group Study.

There are five Daily Devotions following each Group Study. Each devotion has several elements to help students interact with the subject.

See for Yourself

Again, the Bible references are printed in full, though the students are encouraged to highlight or underline the verses in their own Bibles.

Ask Yourself

These questions provide opportunities for students to think through and read closely the Bible passages.

Think for Yourself

This is a section for spiritual journaling to reflect on how the material will make a difference in their lives.

Experience It Yourself

This is a practical exercise to help students act on what they are learning.

Each of these elements are intended to help provide the best learning experience and enhance a student's quiet time with God.

leader AS GUIDE

All small groups need a leader. But that is *leader* as in facilitator and guide, not lecturer or guru. Students will be wrestling with major life issues, and your job is to truly listen to their lives and hear the questions that are only half expressed. You must use the gift of discernment to decide when to step in and answer questions, and when the deeper work should be done in silence.

Remember to let students discuss what they honestly believe and think. The study is designed to put them on a path to discover deeper truths during the five Daily Devotions. At the beginning of each Group Study, use the review questions as a time to draw out what they have discovered. Do not let this degenerate into a "quick-and-easy-answer" time or settle for halfhearted responses like "The week was okay," or "I didn't complete the work." Remind students of the commitment they made at the beginning of the study to grow in Christ. Even though students will have an accountability partner to encourage them during the week, it is highly recommended that you or the small group leader call each student midweek to see how they are doing with their Daily Devotions. This weekly phone call is a very important tool to keep students committed to the *G-Force* study. Remember to encourage students for what they are learning and how they are becoming more like Christ, rather than just affirming them for doing the work.

The following pages cover the main teaching points for each Group Study and Daily Devotion, as well as any sensitive points you may want to cover or look out for. Special materials or props you will need for the Group Study are also listed.

1. Fully DEVOTED

Getting Ready for the Group Study

Materials

▸▸ *Pens.* In this first study students will be asked to sign a pledge committing themselves to this journey. Make sure you have enough pens on hand for every student.

▸▸ *Highlighters.* Give students highlighters to use during the coming weeks so they can highlight verses in their Bibles.

▸▸ *White board.* During the discussion you will need a white board, flip chart, chalkboard, or overhead in order to write down words students come up with.

▸▸ *Candle(s) and matches.* Each group will need a small candle and matches for the Community Time exercise.

▸▸ *Index cards.* Give students eight to ten index cards. They will need these for a variety of activities during the study.

Notes

▸▸ At the end of the study, students pair off and form accountability partnerships. Make sure each student has a partner.

▸▸ Encourage students to take the Daily Devotions seriously and do them throughout the week (rather than waiting until the night before to merely read through them). The value of the devotions isn't just the information they contain but the invitation they extend to experience time with God throughout the week. Students' experiences will be a significant part of the group discussion each time the group meets. Students who actively participate in the Daily Devotions will get a lot more out of the study.

▸▸ Remind students that it will take an average of twenty minutes to complete the Daily Devotions.

Group Study Key Learning
The heart of the Christian life is our spiritual transformation where we become like Jesus.

Daily Devotions Key Learning
1. *Giving Your All:* We must learn to live life as a representative of Jesus.
2. *A Marathon, Not a Sprint:* The Christian life is a race that requires discipline and training.
3. *Graduation:* If we are not growing as Christians, something is wrong.
4. *A Walk with God:* God wants to be our friend.
5. *Be Yourself:* We need to be honest about what we really believe and where we are on our spiritual journey.

2. Grace, PART 1: A TRUE GIFT

Getting Ready for the Group Study
Materials
▸▸ *White board.* During the discussion you will need a white board, flip chart, chalkboard, or overhead in order to write down words students come up with.

Notes
▸▸ The Bible reading is very long. You may want students to take turns reading it.

▸▸ Last week was the first week of Daily Devotions. During the Week in Review discussion, gently explore how it went. Did they do all the devotions? Did they mark up their Bibles?

▸▸ During Devotion 4 of the Daily Devotions that follow this week's study, students will be asked to confess their struggles to a trusted friend or church leader. Alert them that this is coming and encourage them to think about who they might contact: someone who has proven they can keep a confidence and is mature enough to handle what is said.

Group Study Key Learning
Grace describes the fundamental basis of our relationship with God.

Daily Devotions Key Learning
1. *Accepting the Gift:* Grace is not based on our performance or successfully following rules to live by.
2. *A Gift of Freedom:* We don't have to pretend to be good enough to receive God's love.
3. *Noticing the Gift:* Living in grace requires a new way of seeing.
4. *Living with the Gift Every Day:* We are set free to live without fear of not measuring up.
5. *An Everlasting Gift:* Grace is a gift we receive every day for the rest of our lives.

3. Grace, PART 2: SHARING THE GIFT

Getting Ready for the Group Study
Materials
▸▸ *White board.* During the discussion you will need a white board, flip chart, chalkboard, or overhead in order to write down words and ideas students come up with.

▸▸ *Candles and matches.* Each group will need a small candle and matches for the Experience It Together exercise.

▸▸ *Band-Aids.* Students will need a Band-Aid for this week's Daily Devotions. Distribute these at the end of the study.

Group Study Key Learning
God calls all of us to tell others about his amazing gift of grace.

Daily Devotions Key Learning
1. *Being Real:* God uses ordinary, real people like us to show his love to others.
2. *You Have a Story:* Each believer has a unique, powerful story of how God has acted in his or her life. Our personal stories are what those seeking God want to hear.
3. *Telling Your Story:* The friends we know and do life with want to hear our stories because we are people they trust and can relate to. We need to be ready to tell our stories using the three handles of Paul's testimony: before Christ, meeting Christ, after Christ; this can help us to organize our stories.

4. *Growing in Compassion:* We need to grow in compassion for our lost friends and remember that all people matter to God. Meeting the needs of others is an indication of growing to be more like Jesus—loving God and loving others.

5. *One Life at a Time:* Making a difference in our friends' lives begins one life at a time, remembering that becoming a follower of Christ is a process. Our friends are not projects to "win over." Our role is to love them and be examples of following Christ.

4. Growth, PART I: LOVING GOD

Getting Ready for the Group Study
Notes
>> In the last session students were encouraged to focus on someone to share their conversion story with. During the Week in Review, ask how that went. Did they actually talk to the friend they identified? How did the discussion go? What did they learn about spiritual discussions from this experience?

Group Study Key Learning
Spiritual disciplines are training exercises that equip us to know how to have a deeper relationship with God.

Daily Devotions Key Learning
1. *Training Smarter vs. Harder:* Spiritual disciplines are activities that help us gain power in order to live like Jesus taught and modeled.

2. *"Be Silent, and Know That I Am God!":* When we are truly still and silent with our thoughts, and quiet as well with our bodies, then we can create a space to have God speak into our lives.

3. *A Breath Prayer:* Prayer needs to become our instinct, because God is always present with us and wants us to communicate with him.

4. *Bible Meditation:* Scripture is a love letter from God that has the power to transform our lives.

5. *Dream Big:* We need to dream big for God, remembering that God is a big God and has an exciting plan for our lives.

5. Growth, PART 2: LOVING OTHERS

Getting Ready for the Group Study

Notes

▸▸ During the Week in Review, explore whether or not students are making the effort to find quiet places to meet with God. You may want to brainstorm some ideas for where they can go to read Scripture and pray.

Group Study Key Learning

People matter to God. As we know God better, we begin to see the world the way he does—through eyes of love.

Daily Devotions Key Learning

1. *Servant Leader:* Jesus was the ultimate servant leader. His message was clear—if we want to grow to be like him, we must learn to serve others.

2. *The Power of Encouragement:* Simply becoming a person who encourages others can be a powerful gift to others, and an indication that God is transforming our lives.

3. *2:14 Attitude:* If we want to grow to be more like Jesus, we need to learn how to change our attitudes to be positive regardless of our situation.

4. *The Gossip Challenge:* Even with the best of intentions, gossip can damage relationships. For Christ-likeness to grow in us, gossip must subside.

5. *Love of a Different Kind:* The most radical teaching of Jesus is that we are to have courage to show love to others.

6. Groups, PART 1: BUILDING AUTHENTIC COMMUNITY

Getting Ready for the Group Study

Notes

▸▸ During the Week in Review, ask students about their experiences in encouraging others, and about their attitudes—if they became more positive during the week.

Group Study Key Learning

Transformation happens most effectively in the context of small groups.

Daily Devotions Key Learning

1. *The Giver vs. the Taker:* Small groups provide a powerful context for authentic community and for experiencing spiritual growth.

2. *A Giver's Gift: A Listening Ear:* Truly listening and acknowledging what we hear from others is a powerful gift.

3. *It Ain't Easy to Forgive:* All Christ-followers are expected to forgive and reconcile our relationships in order to build strong, healthy communities.

4. *Radical Love:* All people matter to God, regardless of their status or background.

5. *Speaking the Truth in Love:* Living in real community means we have a strong commitment to resolve conflicts by speaking the truth in love.

7. Groups, PART 2: RECEIVING LOVE

Getting Ready for the Group Study
Materials
▸▸ *Colored string or twine.* Students will need colored string or twine this week for their Daily Devotions. Pass these out at the end of the study.

Notes
▸▸ Alert students that next week they need to bring a shoe box with them.

▸▸ Begin now to gather some extra shoe boxes to have available for any students who forget to bring one.

Group Study Key Learning
Healthy community life is dependent on extending and receiving grace.

Daily Devotions Key Learning
1. *No One Stands Alone:* We need to learn how to receive the blessing and help of others with gratefulness and a humble heart.

2. *Let Yourself Be Known:* Being a part of authentic community means being willing to be honest about our fears, weaknesses, and struggle with sin.

3. *Hide-and-Seek:* Being a Christ-follower means that you don't hide your true self from those close to you, knowing that you are never alone and that God is always there for you.

4. *Community Breakers:* If you aren't willing to receive correction from people that care for you and God has put in your life, real community breaks down.

5. *Having the Right Expectations:* Christian friends cannot meet all of our needs and may, in fact, disappoint us. But that should not stop us from experiencing authentic community and showing Christ's love to one another.

8. Gifts, PART 1: DISCOVERING YOUR GIFTS

Getting Ready for the Group Study
Materials

▸▸ *Shoe boxes.* Bring several extra shoe boxes to have available for students who forget theirs. These will be used throughout the next two sessions of studies and devotions.

▸▸ *White paper.* Each student will need a sheet of white paper large enough to wrap and cover the lid of his or her shoe box.

▸▸ *Scissors and tape.* Have scissors and tape on hand for students to use in covering their shoe box lids.

Group Study Key Learning
Spiritual gifts are divine enablements—special abilities God gives to each of his followers.

Daily Devotions Key Learning

1. *Use Me:* Each Christ-follower is responsible to discover and use their spiritual gifts for kingdom work.

2. *Putting the Pieces Together:* A good way to understand what our gifts may be is to look at how God wired us up in special ways to be a difference-maker for him.

3. *Finding the Right Gift:* The Holy Spirit is the one who distributes gifts and decides which gifts each person should have.

4. *Who Am I?:* God knows who we are, and how he made us. And he wants to use us in a powerful way to do his work.

5. *Celebrating Others' Gifts:* We need to learn how to celebrate each other's gifts as well as recognize our own unique gifts.

9. Gifts, PART 2: USING YOUR GIFTS

Getting Ready for the Group Study
Materials

▸▸ *Large puzzle pieces.* Find an inexpensive children's puzzle with large pieces (at least two inches or so). At the end of the Group Study, distribute the puzzle pieces. Students will use them this week during the Daily Devotions.

Group Study Key Learning

When we decide to use our gifts for a common purpose, God can do amazing things.

Daily Devotions Key Learning

1. *The Right Purpose:* Every believer is given at least one spiritual gift for the advancement of God's purpose.
2. *The Right Gift:* God made us the way we are, and intends to use us the way he made us. God did not make a mistake with the gifts he has given us.
3. *The Right Attitude:* No matter how small or large our services are, they're important to God. We are serving God and not humans. The Lord will reward everyone for whatever good they do.
4. *The Right Vine:* Our gifts, to become fruitful, must be nourished in Christ. Without Christ, we can do nothing.
5. *The Church—The Hope of the World:* When we use our spiritual gifts with an attitude of servanthood, a wonderful transformation takes place in us and through us.

10. Good Stewardship, PART 1: SHOW ME THE MONEY

Getting Ready for the Group Study

Materials

>> *Index cards.* Students will need index cards for this week's Daily Devotions. Distribute these at the end of the study.

Group Study Key Learning

Living a life of freedom comes from trusting God as leader, recognizing that everything we've been given is a gift from God.

Daily Devotions Key Learning

1. *Whose Money Is It?:* Now is the time in our lives to begin thinking about and understanding the importance of stewardship with our money.
2. *Debt Free:* There is a big difference between a "want" and a "need." We need to honor God with all he has given us.
3. *Living Large:* God warns us about the trap and harmful effects of desiring money, believing it will bring happiness and fulfillment.
4. *Being a Cheerful Giver:* God wants to see an attitude of joy and compassion in our giving.
5. *The Blessing:* God makes it very clear that he wants to bless his faithful children.

11. Good Stewardship, PART 2: ALL I HAVE IS YOURS, GOD

Getting Ready for the Group Study

Materials

>> *Large index cards.* Students will need index cards for the Experience It Together exercise.

Group Study Key Learning

Good Stewardship involves more than handling our money right, but also our talents, time, and our bodies.

Daily Devotions Key Learning

1. *Having More Than I Need:* God wants us not to forget those who are less fortunate, and to be good stewards of the abundance he has given us.

2. *Time Out:* Time is a gift from God. We need to decide how much time we want to give back in spending time alone with God.

3. *The Perfect Body:* God cares about how we take care of our bodies—not to please people but to honor God. Your body is a temple for the Holy Spirit.

4. *Talented Humility:* The talents God has given us are a way to bring blessing to God and others.

5. *Being a Good Trustee:* In God's kingdom, being a trustee means letting God own all that is his: our money, our possessions, our bodies, our talents, our gifts.